Towards Socialist Welfare Work

Critical Texts in Social Work and the
Welfare State

General Editor: Peter Leonard

Towards Socialist Welfare Work

Working in the State

Steve Bolger, Paul Corrigan,
Jan Docking and Nick Frost

First published 1981 by
THE MACMILLAN PRESS LTD
London and Basingstoke
Associated companies in Delhi Dublin
Hong Kong Johannesburg Lagos Melbourne
New York Singapore and Tokyo

ISBN 0 333 28905 6 (hard cover)
ISBN 0 333 28906 4 (paper cover)

Typeset by STYLESET LIMITED, Salisbury, Wilts.
Printed in Hong Kong

Contents

Editor's Introduction

The first volume in this series was published in 1978, towards what we can now see as possibly the end of a long post-war period of social democratic hegemony. My introduction to that book began with the indisputable assertion that the welfare state was in a condition of profound crisis and I went on to criticise various explanations of the crisis as a preliminary to introducing a series which was to be based upon marxist analyses of the crisis.[1] In the two years which have passed since the series began we have experienced the beginning of a far-reaching change in British politics, namely a concerted effort by the radical right to shift the balance of class forces in this country irrevocably in its direction. There can be little doubt that these radical right forces have been successful in their ideological penetration of sections of the working class and that the consequences for the social democratic welfare state are profound.

The crisis for the welfare state has therefore deepened, as a government committed to fragmenting the working class and subjugating the trade unions has implemented its policies of public expenditure cuts and restructuring. The inauguration of a new form of class rule is accompanied by a set of policies designed to establish a new political and ideological offensive in the heartlands of working-class consciousness.

So far as social policy is concerned, this offensive has important features which distinguish it from the social policy of all previous post-war governments. Whether Labour or Conservative, these governments in practice followed a Keynesian economic and social programme which required the state to be a manager of demand and a provider of welfare as a basic prerequisite for capitalist growth. The organisations and institutions which were established during this period, especially within the field of welfare, all bore to some degree the imprint of social democratic ideology and politics within an overall commitment to capital accumulation and profitability. The various services within the welfare state also reflected the fundamental contradiction of social democracy: on the one hand, an aspiration towards greater equality, on the other, a response to the demand of capital that the social reproduction of class relations shall continue unhindered.

Into this social democratic hegemony in welfare, then, enters the radical right. In social policy it constitutes a planned assault on the benefits, however meagre, which the working class has achieved in the welfare field, based upon an *anti-statist* ideological offensive. The present volume argues that this anti-statism is authenticated in the daily lives of working-class populations, for the welfare state is rarely experienced now as primarily beneficial. As Stuart Hall points out:

> In the absence of any fuller mobilization of democratic initiatives, the state is increasingly encountered and experienced by ordinary working people as, indeed, not a beneficiary but a powerful, bureaucratic imposition. And this experience is not misguided since, in its effective operations with respect to the popular classes, the state is less and less present as a welfare institution and more and more present as the state of 'state monopoly capital'.[2]

The anti-statism of radical right welfare policy is, then, deeply connected to the experiences of the working-class population in its dealings with education, housing, social services and social security. As these experiences are predominantly alienating, a valuable base is established for a right-wing onslaught, not of course on the undemocratic structures of services, but on their level and content. This anti-statism, allied to authoritarian responses to 'law and order' and the reinforcement of institutionalised sexism and racism, provides the foundation for radical right social policy.

As the power of the right appears to increase, the left is presented with a challenge to both theory and practice. In the past, marxist analysis of the welfare state, if it was convincing, had to be based upon a deep critique of the social democratic ideology and practices embedded in the various services. The present book furthers that analysis considerably, but it must be acknowledged that many marxist commentators have failed to distinguish the specifically *social democratic* nature of the welfare state from a general picture of welfare as simply a feature of class exploitation in advanced capitalism. The entry of a right-wing government which attempts to sweep away social democratic institutions in the pursuit of radical change may well encourage more attention to be given, by the left, to the particular contradictions and possibilities contained in these institutions. Certainly, more attention is being given to analyses of class struggle in relation to the state apparatus of welfare. Recently, for example, Norman Ginsburg wrote a book for this series on struggles over social security and housing,[3] whilst the Conference of Socialist Economists has provided a useful survey of the cuts and restructuring undertaken in the 1970s.[4] For the left, a major question becomes: can we use the beleaguered social democratic institutions as part of a wider strategy against the right without being incorporated into social democratic reformist politics?

In the first book in this series, *Social Work Practice under Capitalism*,[5] an attempt was made to begin the process of defining and analysing the possibilities of a practice within the welfare state which was based upon marxist theory and marxist politics. This present book, by Steve Bolger, Paul Corrigan, Jan Docking and Nick Frost, is a direct successor to that first attempt, incubated within the same concerns, similarly committed to working on the contradictions within the welfare state, and continuing the examination of the possibilities of pushing forward class struggle within the state institutions themselves.

A major theme of this book, especially where it examines the practice and structure of social service departments, is the analysis and utilisation of the contradiction between individualisation and collectivisation in welfare operations. So far as social work is concerned, we can identify the commitment that the state has both to collectivise and to individualise social workers. The move towards some collectivisation was intensified by the Seebohm Report: the establishment of 'community-based' area teams in the new social services would, by being closer to the working-class clientele, be more accessible and effective. At the same time the size and complexity of social service departments demanded a degree of decentralisation to local areas within an overall strategy of central control. The other side of the coin is the need continuously to individualise both social work and social workers. Such individualisation serves both to reproduce the ideological legitimation of individual pathology explanations — blaming the individual victim — and also to fragment and control social workers. *Towards Socialist Welfare Work* shows us the possibilities of using this and other contradictions as part of developing a socialist practice in the welfare state, and it does so not by reference to abstract theory or general rhetoric but by a very practical examination of what is feasible. Because the authors are themselves immersed in practice, their prescriptions emerge with particular force.

But the entry of the radical right presents us with a problem. If, as Cynthia Cockburn has argued,[6] local government is simply 'the local state' and so subject to the same imperatives and processes as the central state, will not the radical right's ideology and policies sweep through local government demolishing those institutions which have been erected by working-class social democratic politics? It may be possible to argue that the central state is concerned primarily with *social investment* whereas local authorities have the task of *social consumption*[7] and that therefore there is bound to be contradiction and conflict between these different levels. For its part, *Towards Socialist Welfare Work* argues that the social democratic institutions of local government, however much under pressure, are a suitable arena of struggle both against the radical right and against social democratic reformism in welfare. More positively, the authors propose tactics and strategies which will contribute to the democratisation of welfare services and the eventual development of a socialist consciousness among those involved in welfare operations.

Towards Socialist Welfare Work will, like the previous books in the series, provoke argument and debate. This will be especially so because it is about what workers in the welfare state might actually *do*, rather than simply an analysis of existing structures. Even where the book is concerned with general issues about the welfare state — for example, in its examination of welfare ideologies and its account of the restructuring of capital and the state — it speaks directly to the experience of the worker in the state apparatus. Where it explores specific areas of welfare practice — the area team in social services, child care practice and community work — it cements a deep relationship between theory and practice. Its proposals for socialist welfare work are based upon a careful materialist analysis of the particular problems and possibilities which workers face at this precise point in our history; it shows how an understanding of this history can enable us to use the contradictions in a progressive way.

If *Towards Socialist Welfare Work* leads to socialist experiments in welfare practice and encourages others to dispute with it from the point of view of practice, then, for the authors and for the series editor, it will have served its purpose. In my view, this is a profoundly important book for those who are struggling with the day-to-day problems of practice in the welfare state.

PETER LEONARD

NOTES TO THE EDITOR'S INTRODUCTION

1. See especially Ian Gough, *The Political Economy of the Welfare State* (London: Macmillan, 1979).
2. Stuart Hall, 'The Great Moving Right Show', *Marxism Today*, January 1979.
3. Norman Ginsburg, *Class, Capital and Social Policy* (London: Macmillan, 1979).
4. CSE State Group, *Struggle over the State: cuts and restructuring in contemporary Britain* (CSE Books, 1979).
5. Paul Corrigan and Peter Leonard, *Social Work Practice under Capitalism: a Marxist Approach* (London: Macmillan, 1978).
6. Cynthia Cockburn, *The Local State* (London: Pluto Press, 1977).
7. See P. Saunders, 'Local Government and the State', *New Society*, 13 March 1980.

Introduction

This book aims to make a practical and theoretical contribution to the struggle to develop socialist forms of practice within the apparatus of the welfare state. In writing the book we have had two primary audiences in mind. First, we are concerned to develop an analysis which is important to the mass of welfare workers as they face the day-to-day problems of their work. Secondly, we attempt to reach socialists involved in other forms of struggle in order to point to the importance of struggles within the welfare state.

We have not produced a finished blueprint. What we have attempted to do is to understand developments in the welfare state and to point to the practice possibilities which have grown from these developments.

Our particular object of study are those British state apparatuses collectively known as the 'welfare state'. Our analysis of these apparatuses is placed squarely within the context of the British capitalist social formation. We hope that one day this book will be read with a wry smile by welfare workers and will have only historical significance. Until then, however, the context and recurring theme of this book is the welfare state in a capitalist social formation.

The title of this study contains three components which must be understood independently and collectively. The first component, *towards*, illustrates a movement and relates to a progressive process. The second, *socialist*, relates to a form of society and a form of practice. The third, *welfare work*, is a type of work which is usually seen as a service.

In using this title we are attempting to contribute to the

reconstruction of a tradition; that tradition which has seen 'welfare' and 'socialism' as having a lot in common. The reconstruction of this tradition cannot fully take place without a revolutionary change in the social relationships of our social formation. In other words this book is *not* saying that socialist welfare work can be fully achieved in our society as presently constituted. *But neither* are we saying that it is impossible to struggle for socialist forms of welfare practice within capitalist society. Many of the forms of the welfare state contain within them socialist forms but they lack a consistent material base. That is to say, they are built on the ebb and flow of the class struggle. We see socialism as providing that material base, which means that welfare provision can be built on a solid political, economic, ideological base.

This book sees the state apparatus as the major arena where these struggles will take place. This is not necessarily the case with all societies, at all times in history. However in Great Britain in the 1980s the state is a crucial centre for struggle around welfare issues. Social democracy has constructed a massive welfare apparatus within the state.

This was not the only possibility — working-class people have made attempts to construct their own welfare apparatus, as the history of the friendly societies and independent trade unions illustrates. However, when there has been a universal service to provide — be it education, pensions or Factory Acts — the working class has had to turn to the state.

The expansion of the state in welfare activities has been matched by the expansion of state activities in other arenas. The central analytic part of this book looks at the way the state changed in the 1960s and 1970s (a process that we refer to as restructuring). This period saw changes in all those parts of the state in which welfare workers struggle. All of us within the welfare state have simple *experienced* this process: this study is an attempt to understand and struggle with it.

The aim of this book is to point to a way in which we can become a conscious part of a struggle to change welfare. A change that will only happen in a progressive direction if it is fully linked to organisations of working people, and will only really last if it becomes a part of the struggle for a socialist Britain.

THE FORM OF THE BOOK

Chapter 1 is a discussion of various ideologies of welfare. This is not an attempt to provide an exhaustive analysis of different theories of welfare, rather it attempts to underpin the other sections on structure, practice and politics that follow. Nor is the chapter intended to discuss theory as such; rather it is about ideologies — the ideologies that construct and interfere with our practice; the ideologies that structure the organisations we work for; the ideologies that in some cases win elections. Of course we will attempt to relate such ideologies of welfare to recognised theories, but the chapter aims principally to uncover the ideas that people struggle with.

Chapter 2 is a discussion of the nature of changes in the state in the UK, focusing in particular on the structures in which welfare workers struggle. It is intended to illustrate that the structures we live in are *made*, that they have been con-structed as a result of specific struggles. More than this we hope to show that all these structures (Mrs Thatcher notwith-standing) are made within the ideology and practice of social democracy and that this ideology contains a number of important contradictions.

It is important for us to pause for a moment here to explore the idea of *contradiction*, since much of the book is built around the concept. This may seem odd to the reader, since in common parlance for a person to admit that their argument is built around a contradiction is to admit that they have a major problem in their argument, that they are not really consistent. For us, and for most marxists, the concept of contradiction within social structures is essential. A contradic-tion within a structure must not be confused with a difference between one structure and another. A contradiction means that there are elements of that structure that can only be *fully* realised, can only be put into effect, by destroying other elements of that structure. This means that the structure is in *constant tension*, since simultaneously one part of the struc-ture can only be successfully realised at the expense of another.

One contradiction that we discuss at length in Chapter 3 appears within social service departments between individualised experiences of work for the welfare worker and team work. As we say, most people experience the former as dominant and the latter as a niggling problem. We will contend that for political reasons at the time, this specific form of *structure* had to be built around this contradiction; it had to reflect the recognition that an area team in a social service department had to exist *as a team*. But also that the prime mode of work was still to exist at the level of individual work.

This example, and the mode of analysis, is crucial since many of us are given to statements which neglect this understanding of contradiction. 'Social service departments are inevitably about individualised work'; 'social work is about oppression.' Such statements reflect a simple search for certainty away from the fact that social institutions are built around contradictions.

We are suggesting that all welfare state structures contain a series of contradictions. We see these contradictions as being constructed by the struggle between the working class and monopoly capital, and this we see as the *primary* contradiction. This means that we all work in institutions that are riven, in their very structure, with contradictions. This is important. If for example we were to see a person working with children in a social service department as working in a structure which had a clear, direct, unilinear aim (say social control), then that worker would have a very difficult time doing anything else. Similarly if a welfare worker was in a structure that was totally, unremittingly individualist then it would be difficult to work in a way that was anything but individualistic. We will be suggesting that the structure of welfare work has been made around a contradiction. This has not been done by accident, but has come about in the first instance because of the nature and extent of class struggle in the UK.

In Chapter 2 we specifically look at the changing British state from the 1960s to the present day. We do this because over this period nearly every aspect of the state has undergone a massive set of changes. We see these changes as springing from factors that have themselves sprung from the economic problems experienced by capital in the UK. We choose these dates not simply because they represent the beginning of a period of state change, but also the early 1960s saw the beginning of the recognition of severe economic crises.

In the next three chapters we try to link this analysis with some specific problems of welfare work. The logic of this relationship is contained in the theory of state change that we use to analyse these large state changes. For, if the contradiction of the service and the organisation within which we work has been originally constructed by class struggle, then it is inevitable that it will only be resolved through relating our work within the welfare state to that wider struggle.

First we look at the site, the actual arena within which the bulk of statutory welfare work is carried out, the area organisation of the social service department. Through looking closely at the Seebohm Report and the ensuing reorganisation we explore the precise contradiction between individualism and collectivism as it has been structured into the service. We stand for the collective approach in terms of both service provision and the workers' experience of that service provision. We stand for this not only because we like 'groups' above 'individualism' but because it is through such a collective approach that organisations of working people can have a more democratic say in the provision and running of the service. In this section we discuss the experiences of different forms of collective activity that welfare workers have had during a recent period of trade union activity. Here the same people, welfare workers, who often find collective work so difficult, managed to construct a real set of group experiences which in some cases achieved a great deal.

Secondly we look at child care and specifically at the statutory aspects of child care and the way in which a progressive person works in that area. We pick such an arena because a large percentage of qualified social workers' time is spent within it, and because it is a statutory area of work, which appears to have little room for manoeuvre or change in the realm of day-to-day practice. We also pick this area to try to demonstrate that even in close relationship to the law itself, welfare is built around contradictions; laws do not have unilinear meanings but can represent contradictions that may in turn provide some room for manoeuvre themselves.

Thirdly in this section we look at the emergence and practice of community work in Britain since the late 1960s.

Community work has been seen by some as clearly a progressive form of welfare work, and by others more critically as a 'device' to further incorporate working-class struggle at home and in the community; we try to show how the structure of the work ensures that it can move towards either of these functions depending on the way in which alliances are constructed and the work is carried out. Again we stress the way in which community politics have a vast and important role to play in any form of progressive struggle.

Thus, we will examine three practical areas of welfare work; we will explore the way in which 'progressive' welfare workers have tried to construct a different form of work and try to see how that work can be defended and extended. Given the overall analysis we will stress the necessity of creating links and alliances around these issues from 'inside' the state to 'outside'. That is with organisations that exist outside of the boundaries of the state. Such a strategy has of course often been discussed, but in our final section we will explore the direct way in which such alliances car influence and extend 'progressive' work within the state; how they can ensure that such progressive work has a direct class experience and a direct class political link; how that experience can be inextricably interwoven with the wider struggle for socialism; how a better way of working with children in care forms a major part of that struggle for socialist revolution.

The totality of this argument is constructed *not* around the separate sections but around their relationships. The following section on ideology is only rendered fully understandable in relationship to a specific understanding of the state in the UK in the 1960s and 1970s. Similarly, that can only be made sense of by the specifics of the third section and the political directions of the conclusions. Obviously, this is a political book; it is meant to be about directions of work, it is meant to be about struggle and change. Being a socialist, struggling for socialist political work and moving towards socialist practice is not a simple straightforward process. We are suggesting that the conditions constructed by social democracy in the UK not only allow us as socialists to write this book, but also to struggle towards socialist welfare work as a possibility.

1
Ideologies of Welfare

Most social science books and nearly all books about welfare are written as if the writers had purged themselves of all their values, of all their politics. Similarly, much welfare work is carried out in a strange 'objective' environment, where people make 'objective' decisions based on 'objective' data. Policies are constructed on objective administrative criteria — cuts and expansion occur, and always for the best.

Occasionally this whole facade is challenged: a home is closed, an old person freezes to death; the army is expanded and home helps are cut. Suddenly it begins to look as though welfare is about values after all, but then the facade is re-established and there is a return to a calm objectivity.

We believe that claims of objectivity in welfare are a complete myth. Objectivity as a definition of events is imposed and constructed by dominant social practices, and will, in fact, take different forms at different historical stages. For example, it may be an objective truth that the majority of people aspire to owning their own house. However, this is a 'truth' constructed and reinforced by a whole series of major ideological institutions — the family, the Inland Revenue, the building societies, political parties, and so on. It is a truth constructed in a specific historical space and in the interests of specific social classes. In these circumstances ideology seems to disappear and 'truth' emerges in its place.

Such truths are historically fragile. Whilst it is possible to eradicate differences over brief historical periods such positions cannot be maintained for any great length of time. In the field of welfare, the late 1970s and the 1980s mark a time when truths have been shattered and it is now possible to point to the ideological basis of any position and any argument. What we hope to do in this section is outline what we see as the major ideological positions on welfare and also outline our own position. Importantly most of us operate for much of the time in a 'hotch-potch' of different ideological positions. Thus the following outlines are meant to provide insights not only into other people's positions but also to elucidate some of the ideas behind our own. What does this mean? None of us operate singlemindedly on the basis of one of these major ideologies all the time. This is especially true of people who actually conduct their understanding of welfare within the rough and tumble world of practice. This section is trying to tease out the major strands in these different positions so that we can better understand our disagreements, both between each other and within our own position.

Such a task is an essential prerequisite for any of us who really want to direct our practice in a self-conscious way. Indeed many people in welfare work seem to believe at the moment that there is a simple relationship between theory and practice in the work. That all you have to do is work out the theory and then put it into effect. Our response to this is that much of our existing and future practice is dominated by a variety of different positions. We feel it is vital to aim for a more dominant, more directed relationship between theory and practice but also that reading or writing a book will not revolutionise all the problems involved.

We are saying that an *essential* prerequisite for all those interested in moving towards a socialist welfare practice is to understand the ideologies that construct the individual parts of our practice — be it progressive, traditional, or just plain confused. First, we will illustrate the various major ideologies that dominate the practice and policies of welfare, and demonstrate that ideologies are not external but are very much a part of us. Second, we intend to put forward the ideology of this book in order to illustrate how we envisage socialists in welfare moving forward.

To this end we explore initially three ideologies, which we have designated as social democracy, Thatcherism and democratic socialism. In using these directly political designations we hope to illustrate that ideologies do not exist as 'ideas' alone, but also as social practices. Ideologies have a concrete existence in the practices that make up a social formation. It is therefore also the case that these ideologies exist as sites of political conflict and therefore not in any 'ideal form'.

SOCIAL DEMOCRACY AND WELFARE – 'THE MOVING FRONTIER OF SOCIAL CONSCIENCE'

> At one extreme are those who regard the social services as a charitable burden borne on the back of the 'productive' institutions of the economy. At the other extreme are those who regard these services as a necessary and growing feature of a 'progressive' economy, producing an increasingly just and efficient society in which the major decisions will be based on rational and humane criteria. (Donnison and Chapman, 1975, p. 16)

It is important to note that as far as Donnison and Chapman are concerned, in 1975 these two positions represented the extremes of possibility. We will deal with the first extreme in its political form when discussing Thatcherism; what is important here is the second extreme. This point of view dominated the politics of welfare institutions and practice for over thirty years. Social democracy provided the basis for the building of the post-war social services and, until 3 May 1979, dominated all major institutions within it. Whole institutions within society, whole sub-disciplines within social sciences have been constructed in the image of social democracy.

It is vital to stress that social democracy plays this dual function in dominating welfare. At one and the same time, it is structured into the *fabric* of institutions through social policy, as well as being an ideology used to *study* those institutions. Thus it has constructed a dominant position both in terms of practical institutions *and* in terms of making sense of those institutions. Alongside of this it has been within the ideology of social democracy, again until 1979, that the dominant form of political discussion about welfare has taken place.

Therefore we are talking about an impressively strong

ideology; and one that is all the more difficult to discuss because of its all-powerful nature. If something constructs the places we work in, the 'training' that we receive, the ideas we read in the paper, the parameters of our discussions, then it becomes like part of the wallpaper, something we take entirely for granted. Any of us are at fault if we believe that we operate completely outside of social democracy.

Social democracy distances itself from those elements of capitalist society which it finds irrational and anti-humanistic. It believes that it is not necessary for people to go hungry, to be homeless or uneducated. Crucially, social democracy believes that these problems can be alleviated within capitalism, albeit a reformed and more humane capitalism. The classic British social democrats — Crosland, Gaitskell and Titmuss — believed that in the final analysis it was necessary to come to an accommodation with capitalist society. Their concept of change does not include the abolition of the crucial features of capitalism — the production of surplus value, wage labour, and so on. They are however all committed to reform and to change, and they see the welfare apparatuses of society as the main agents of change. Welfare is posed *against* the institutions of the market; humanistic values posed against those of capitalism. What does this mean?

First, that these institutions contain within them different social relations than either those of customer/seller or worker/employer. They are constructed around some aspect of one section of the community looking after another, weaker, poorer, less well off section. This is not expressed in a charitable way but in terms of the rights and duties of sections of the population. Secondly, it believes that the problems and difficulties of poorer, weaker people can actually be either ameliorated or solved within this form of society. That is, the point of intervention is actually to solve certain problems experienced by people. Third, the main instrument to carry out this policy is the state. The state can be posed against the market as a strong institution within which these different, 'welfare' sets of social relations can be constructed. It is essential then to ensure that a political battle is waged actually to make these institutions. This political battle takes place almost exclusively in two ways. First, major political changes come through the ballot box, the election of a radical/welfare government either at Westminster or at local authority level being an important step in setting up any welfare institution. Second, we involve ourselves in pressure groups which put forward a point of view about a service; these consist either of professional workers actually doing the job, or clients.

Change comes about, by affecting the civil service and 'public opinion' on issues, by underlining the humanitarian/conscience side of the welfare aspects of institutions, by appealing to people's 'better nature'.

However, social democracy is not completely naive: it recognises that the major institutions and values of society still exist and assumes that they will for all time. These institutions and values are a part of 'the facts of life' which must be taken into account in formulating proposals. Consequently we must, for example, make sure that all our plans are costed and can be argued for in terms of cost-benefit analysis. We must also make sure that our plans and ideas in the arena of 'law and order' are argued for in such a way as to prove that this will eradicate crime quicker than the older authoritarian methods. Social democracy will only win any particular policy argument by making sure that its case is 'rational'.

Thus at every stage it is arguing its case in terms of the rationality of the more humane capitalist values. This is the only way in which social democracy sees itself as coming to terms with the consistent continuation of capitalist values and institutions. Coming to terms with reality and yet at all times being on the defensive about any progress being made or any real change taking place is a central stance of social democracy. This places social democratic views of welfare in a subordinate position when arguing against capitalist values; it then becomes essential for us to win the arguments to go forward.

Of course, social democratic views of welfare change over time. At certain times there is a vision of the future in which welfare will have fully established itself and will not be subordinate to capitalist values and institutions. Perhaps these visions overtake people in the first three months of a Labour government; but for most of the time and especially in the late 1970s social democratic views of welfare have been in retreat and in a state of some considerable disarray.

The crucial feature here is the social democratic conception of politics. The Labour Party in Great Britain has failed to construct a democratic relationship between the state welfare apparatus and the working class. Welfare reforms are imposed from 'above' for the good of ordinary people. They are then run by professionals who have only a tenuous democratic responsibility to the mass of the people through elected representatives. We can detect a social democratic fear of the working class — a fear that they are not actually capable of being involved in the administration of state services. In fact this probably reflects a more fundamental fear that the working class is racist, sexist and individualist and does not actually want the state services that are being imposed on it!

Social democracy also has similar effects within its own party organisation. First, the membership of the whole party is only mobilised around electoral issues and issues of internal party organisation. These factors tend to move the *party* but bear little relationship to the mass of the people. Secondly, this electoralism is reflected in the status given to elected representatives within the party: their power *over* elected party officials.

These factors help us to understand the electoral defeat of the Labour Party on 3 May 1979. We must understand that this defeat was a rejection by a large portion of the working class of the state services that social democracy had built but for which it had manifestly failed to provide a sound democratic base.

What does social democratic ideology mean for workers within the state apparatus? First, it means that most of the institutions in which we work are constructed within this ideology. They are constructed out of 'social conscience'; but they are also constructed in a subordinate relationship with the major capitalist institutions. Thus, whilst social security was formed to help give a decent standard of living to the poorer sections of the population, it is simultaneously essential that people on supplementary benefit or the 'dole' should not feel free of the pressures of the labour market. The means test and stigma must go hand in hand with benefits or the institution will not operate within the boundaries of capitalist social relations.

This book is mainly about the state as a set of apparatuses to work in and to struggle over. By and large social democrats will find this book extremely puzzling, since they see most of the changes instituted in the state before 3 May 1979 as neutral: they see places within which they work as *just* providing a service. This ties in with their view of political struggle, which sees those who 'win power' at elections as then being able to wield full control of all of these services. Welfare workers who are interested in politics should really be involved only in the evenings, at weekends or more likely once a year through a ballot box. They should see politics as a separate issue kept aside from their practice, and they should carry out that side of their lives as 'citizens' *not* as welfare workers. This view sees practitioners joining professional groups and associations to act as pressure groups, or occasionally forming a client pressure group to change policy.

Thus there are channels within social democracy for practitioners to effect and to change policy, but it is important that their actual *work* is kept neutral and depoliticised. Indeed the continual social democratic 'wail' — 'This is not a political matter' — makes this point.

Since this is also a book for those interested in socialist politics as well as aspects of welfare work, it is important to underline some of the wider elements of social democracy. Large numbers of working people believe in social democracy as their political ideology. They see, as the people experiencing 'the problems', that social democracy organises some form of state solution for them. They experience this solution as a direct contradiction; because while they are relieved that something is being done about, say, a pension for their old age, they also experience that pension not only as humiliatingly inadequate to live on but also they have no direct say in how it is administered and run. So for the mass of working people, social democracy is a 'good thing' because it seems to look after the weak and the sick; but it is a 'bad thing' because when you actually need one of the welfare services it is bureaucratic and inadequate as an experience.

Equally, social democrats involved in welfare politics have

a distanced relationship from both the working class and its organisations. They feel that working people are not really to be trusted to hold values of welfare, kindness and integration. They point to the 'greed' of trade unions; the sectionalism of this or that aspect of working-class organisations; and to the materialism of people. As we have said this represents one of the major reasons for the continued subordination of social democracy to capitalism because welfare social democrats seem to be afraid that working people will in fact spurn the values of welfare; as a consequence the repository of welfare values is the 'professional liberal'. Social democrats are instilled with the belief that the politics of welfare should be concealed as much as possible from working people. This in turn leads to the construction of a political elite, as well as of a practice elite.

THATCHERISM AND WELFARE – 'THE WELFARE STATE IS EVIL'

In the section on social democracy we tried to show the subordinate position of social democrats' belief in welfare to what they see as the inevitable facts of life of capitalist values and institutions. The ideology of Thatcherism stops seeing these values as unfortunate facts of life, and sees them as progressive, important and correct aspects of society. Welfare is allowed to exist only in so far as it does not obstruct these values in financial, moral or political terms.

We entitle this particular ideology 'Thatcherism' not because Margaret Thatcher invented it or indeed is even its most articulate exponent; rather we see her as a politician who managed clearly to achieve the first radical change in the politics of welfare since the war. She achieved this in the 1979 election on the back of a steady swing to the right over a long period of time. It is Margaret Thatcher who has placed welfare at the centre of the political and ideological stage; it is Margaret Thatcher who has popularised and organised a whole current of opinion against the bureaucratisation of the social democratic state; it is Margaret Thatcher who achieved a vote of 13½ million people against that welfare state.

Neither Keynesianism nor Monetarism win votes in the electoral market place. But in the doctrines and discourses of 'social market values' — the restoration of competition and personal responsibility for effort and reward, the image of the over-taxed individual, enervated by welfare coddling, his initiative sapped by handouts by the state — 'Thatcherism' has found a powerful means of popularising the principles of a Monetarist philosophy; and in the image of welfare 'scavenger' a well-designed folk devil. (Hall, 1979, p. 17).

What does Thatcherism mean as an ideology of welfare? It seeks to replace all those institutions which have been founded on the belief that the state should take responsibility for aspects of people's lives. It does not just see these institutions as failing; it sees them as 'wrong', not just 'wrong' for the better off in society but 'wrong' for the people who receive them and 'wrong' for the whole of society. Quite genuinely it sees the over-extension of welfare state activities as sapping not only the financial and political will of the nation but also destroying the morality of the individuals involved. The crucial values of incentive and self-help are not only portrayed as values for the market place, but are seen as essential aspects of a morality in every aspect of life.

Consequently 'Thatcherites' see the collapse of British society and economy as having been constructed around the 'over-coddling' and expensive intervention of the welfare apparatuses of the state. For the most part they believe it will take decades fully to dismantle the 'dependence' and to turn back these institutions and values, and that this is the strategy for a 'better future'.

Obviously such an ideology has a direct impact upon the provision of welfare; quite simply it marches through welfare state institutions cutting them to the bone, not simply to save money, but to save people, morality and the future of British enterprise. This obviously has a direct and day-to-day impact on the practice of welfare workers and reconstructs services in an entirely different way to any cuts imposed by social democrats to save money. This is because this exercise carries with it a coherent ideology of *different* ways of providing services. For the most part they argue that the market should be responsible for providing many services. As people's dependence upon the state diminishes, the market will be able to run more and more of the welfare apparatuses of the state. Again it must be stressed that such an approach actually helps people by reducing their dependence and helping them look after themselves, rather than compounding their degradation through a treadmill of increasing clientship.

Alongside of this increasingly residual welfare aspect of the state there will exist, to a varying degree as circumstances dictate, a tough, ideologically reliable, interventionist law and order policy. Thatcherism then does have a positive approach towards many of the existing activities of welfare work. For example, a detailed attitude to most statutory child care work is being developed. In the wish to see the confused liberalism surrounding the law and juveniles demystified by a clear return to justice and the law, a return to the ideology of deterrence as the way in which the courts should deal with offenders is being advanced.

Similarly within the field of social security. It is vitally important that those on social security during sickness and unemployment should be worse off than those in work. This of course is difficult since the overall Thatcher economic policy also involves falling real wages. Consequently, as in the Poor Law of 1834, it is necessary to make some aspect of being on social security much worse than being at work; this is essential since the financial gap will not be as large as could be wished. This will mean reinforcing the 'scrounger-bashing' ideology.

Thus, although it is true that Thatcher is attacking the welfare state, since those services are themselves founded upon contradictions between welfare and capitalist ethics, she can in fact pose herself quite correctly as only attacking *some* aspects of welfare, namely the 'excesses' of social democracy.

DEMOCRATIC SOCIALISM — 'THE WELFARE STATE IS AN ARENA OF CLASS STRUGGLE'

In contrast to both Thatcherism and social democracy we

would now want to develop our own model of welfare. We see this as a model informed by marxism and before exploring it further we want to discuss some appearances of marxism as a political theory in welfare.

There is no doubt that marxism has a distinctive image in welfare that derives from a particular brand of marxism. We would want to disagree with this not simply for the sake of disagreement but to show that actual debate exists within marxism. It is not a monolithic theory.

Marxism has been typified as a stance that is a little too far away, and this is in relation to a marxism that simply dismisses the individual injuries inflicted upon people who live under capitalism as impossible to solve without an overall revolution. Occasionally such a theory has seemed 'heartless' and also, practically for welfare workers, 'useless'. What is its basis?

There is an overall stress upon the power that a capitalist system as an overall society has upon the lives of people in it. There is an equal stress, through a theory of the state, on the impossibility of actions by welfare workers to do anything but act in 'the interests of capital' in that society. Thus it was felt that the stress upon the societal cause of social problems left the nature of welfare intervention at the structural level: at the level of massive political and social change. Indeed, many of us would recognise this as one of the basic tenets held by many of the marxists that we come across in welfare work. 'There is nothing that can be done by tinkering with individual or familial social relationships.' 'All such activities are diversionary/reformist and detract from the real political struggle.'

This book sets itself firmly against such dichotomies between working with individuals and political/revolutionary work. As such we try and explain our position in the remainder of the book. Here we want to defend the fact that it is a *marxist* position and yet disagrees with others who view marxism in a different way.

Similarly when we look at the welfare state: there is a marxist view which sees that state as simply reproducing the social relationships necessary for the interests of capital. It sees the state as an organisation run purely in the interests of monopoly capital, welfare work being posed as 'the iron fist in the velvet glove'. Consequently welfare workers have learnt that marxism sees their work and their practice as purely acting out the interests of capital. Indeed, recently such a view has become quite popular amongst welfare workers themselves; they fear that nothing at all humanistic or welfare orientated *is* actually possible within their job. This form of marxism provides some limited theoretical backing for this position. This has led to some popularity, not for the whole corpus of marxist knowledge, but for those aspects of it which tell the welfare worker that no real substantial advances can be made in the field of welfare work. Again we stand firm against this brand of marxism; we see the state as a set of contradictions caused by the class struggle of society, not as a monolith.

Thirdly, marxism has a reputation for seeing a simple split between revolution and reform. Such a view not only sees the actual work of welfare as inevitably structured by the needs of capital but sees the politics of welfare — the sorts of politics that most welfare workers might struggle to become engaged in — as being a reformist diversion. The dichotomy between reform and revolution is drawn as a sharp distinction by some marxists; a distinction which leaves little possibility for political struggle within a capitalist society, little possibility for building up class confidence or constructing socialism within the corpse of the capitalist order. This book tries to point to the socialist possibilities of welfare politics within a social democratic capitalist setting.

We discuss these three aspects of a form of marxism in order to distance ourselves from some of the images and realities of marxism that welfare workers come across. We do so not to attack those that hold these views but to try to point out our comradely differences.

It is a mistake, therefore, to see marxism as a monolithic theory. The last decade has seen a flowering of marxist theory together with its development as a dynamic and relevant set of ideas which can act as a guide to progressive forms of political practice. In contrast to social democracy we would like to put forward a form of marxist thought and politics which directly informs day-to-day welfare work.

We designate our approach democratic socialism — so illustrating our commitment to the democratic organisation of both the struggle for socialism and the socialist form of society itself.

One of the primary areas where marxist thought has flourished in the last few years has been in its understanding of the state. The importance of the state in the continuation of a capitalist society has been stressed by many writers, particularly in relation to welfare work. Stressing as it does the nature of state work and state struggle, it represents the starting-point of our analysis. Marxists have moved a long way from the conception of the state and its apparatus as the monolithic expression of the will of the dominant economic class. Most notably the late Nicos Poulantzas, amongst others, has emphasised the constitutive role of the class struggle in determining the form and organisation of the state apparatus. The state cannot be viewed as a monolith, since each institution and initiative must be understood in terms of the class struggle going on around it. We would argue that when looking at British society in this century the working class have always had a role to play in some aspects of these struggles — even though the form and content of this involvement will be different in different cases. Consequently we see these state apparatuses as constructed directly under the influence of class struggle and not simply by the ruling class.

The advances made by marxism in this area of analysis have informed and have been informed by the political struggles around the state. It has enabled marxists, sometimes after a considerable period of time, to understand the real significance of the women's struggle amongst other political movements. These struggles are now increasingly seen as central both to socialist politics and socialist construction. Much marxist thought no longer exclusively poses the economic struggle as the sole arbiter of revolutionary politics.

The state is therefore an arena in which class struggles take place. The struggles within and around the state cannot be seen in isolation — each will involve alliances between the working class *within* and the working class *outside* the state.

This probably represents the single most important theoretical message for state workers contained within this book, namely, that your work in the state is work within a structure that has been and will be constructed by class struggle. This is a struggle in which you as an individual and you as a group of welfare workers can play a significant part, *both* as state workers and as a part of class struggle outside of your work. These struggles can draw in many people not usually associated with the working class (such as management in social service departments) on the side of the working class – the exact form of each alliance depending on the nature of each struggle.

However, most of this book looks specifically at the welfare apparatuses of the state, and we make specific claims about these parts of the state and the work carried out within them. If we look at an example, perhaps our analysis will become clear. In the period 1939 to 1949 there was a great deal of change within the welfare apparatuses of the British state. How would we explain these changes? We would see World War Two and the Labour government that followed as reflecting a change in the nature and form of class struggle in this country. The war, given its nature as a total war, had to grant more power to working people in the state and in their lives. We were fighting for 'democracy' and the phrase had to mean something for the people fighting the war; it had to represent not simply an ideal but an experienced reality. 'Full employment', 'an end to want', etc. became necessary parts of the war effort. In these circumstances there is no doubt that working people had more power; they had to be granted new forms of state organisations and higher real wages.

Thus the overall struggle for welfare is one in which the working class actually made significant advances. However, in the construction and operation of the institutions and politics of welfare, the working class has had little direct say. This is the case because they put their political faith in 'experts' to work out the details for them. As we will see in Chapter 2, this represents a familiar form of politics, one wherein the working class may determine the overall direction of change, but be politically absent from the creation of particular policies, the specific direction of which has not been ensured.

We see therefore, the welfare apparatuses of the state as directly constructed by the nature of the class struggle, but we would go beyond this. These apparatuses are absolutely crucial to both the major classes in British society. We stress this point because, by and large, revolutionary socialists have neglected their central role. Recent years, those since the first round of public expenditure cuts, have seen a much greater interest in welfare struggles; a flowering not only of struggle but also of analysis. Why then are welfare politics so important to the class struggle in Britain?

As far back as the 1840s members of the ruling class and their civil servants saw clearly the vital nature *for them* of state intervention in welfare. Edwin Chadwick and others stressed the way in which capitalism as experienced at that time was actually destroying the working class. This was meant not as a metaphor but as a reality; people were being killed off in the cities at a faster rate than they were reproducing themselves. This represented a problem for capital as a whole and they saw the importance of state intervention to ensure the survival of the labour force. At the same time working people realised that there were forms of state intervention that would stop them from dying or from leading such brutalised lives. They struggled for these forms of intervention and expenditure. Consequently welfare interventions *of one form or another* became central to both the capitalist class and the working class. Ever since then there has been a struggle over the *form* of welfare that has resulted. This struggle has contained different conceptions of welfare and has embraced different policies. We have already outlined the ideology and politics of social democracy, stressing its importance as the ideology espoused by the working class in its struggle for welfare. On occasions this ideology has informed the actions in the welfare arena of the capitalist class as well — for example in the field of redundancy, where the Redundancy Payments Act was part of a social democratic advance for the working class — but it also made it possible for monopoly capital to shed a great many more jobs, with less of a fightback against redundancy. We explain more fully in the next chapter how social democracy represents an ideology which contains class struggle inside it.

We are saying then that welfare state apparatuses are central to both classes and are therefore central to political activity. This is important when we turn to the way in which we see the concept of class itself. There is a tendency within marxist thought towards presenting a narrow definition of the working class as those workers employed in productive labour, that is, those directly employed by private capital. There are important debates about whether this includes white-collar workers.

In contrast to this we take a broad definition of what constitutes the working class. It is one that has great importance for welfare workers and clients since it includes them within this class. We see all those who are wage labourers or those who have only their labour power to sell as being a part of the working class. Such a definition is based upon Marx's view that the social relations of production are the defining elements of what constitutes a class. Thus an unemployed worker does not stop being a member of the working class because s/he is not employed at that moment. S/he still only has her/his labour power to sell. Similarly with those who work at home in domestic labour; they only have their labour power to sell and this effects the whole of their life.

In the same way, we would see welfare workers, who also have only their labour power to sell, as members of the working class. These classes only exist in relation to other classes. In other words, the working class only exists at all as a creation of the bourgeoisie; as a consequence of the fact that the bourgeoisie needs labour power. And of course, vice versa, since people who only have their labour power to sell are in direct contrast to those who have other sources of wealth and economic power. It is the consequences of this powerlessness that welfare workers have to deal with on a day-to-day basis.

This broad definition of class means that the relationships between welfare workers, manual industrial workers and welfare clients are relationships *within* a class and not between classes. This is not to say, however, that one day all these groups of people will suddenly wake up and realise that they are part of the same class. Such a consciousness will only come by a long process of detailed struggle.

There are also times, though, when we have to look for class *alliances*, that is, alliances between classes such as the working class and the *petit bourgeoisie*. For example in the struggle against racism and fascism, the *petit bourgeois*, shopkeepers and the owners of small firms play a crucial role. It was this class that formed the crucial power base for Mussolini, Hitler, Franco and the Chilean Junta. If the working class fails to work with it in a useful way then it will be forced to defend its interests against monopoly capital on its own, and these may be represented against the working class. Let us look at two concrete examples. In many community struggles the relationship between the *petit bourgeoisie* and the working class is crucial. Shopowners, vicars, privately employed architects, doctors and owners of small firms are all part of inner-city community struggles. In some cases, unless working people forge an alliance with this group they will run their own struggle in their own way with their own base, *and in their own interests.*

At the time of writing the Thatcher government is discussing a plan to switch the payment of sickness benefit from the state to the employer. The trade union movement is opposed to this and so are a number of small businesses as it is this section which will be hit hardest. Without the involvement of the trade union movement it is possible that such businessmen would move against the whole idea of sickness benefit thereby bringing it into conflict with the trade union movement but into agreement with the government. However, an alliance between these two groups may be central to the retention of sickness benefit within the state's ambit.

Thus we have a conception of state policy and state work as being formed by class struggle and a conception of the working class as being a broad part of the British population. Much of this may be dismissed by some on the 'left' as 'reformist' since it deals with the social relationships of a society constructed by capitalist ethics and force. We feel that the relationship between struggle with a capitalist society and the struggle for socialism goes beyond the simple reform/revolution dichotomy. We believe wholeheartedly in the absolute necessity for a revolution in British society. It is only when that revolution has been fully completed that the welfare services essential to working people will be *either* fully protected *or* able to relate in a fully democratic way to the lives of working people.

However, we see this revolution as a political process that takes place over a long period of time and involves many people in many struggles. These struggles need to involve working-class people in taking more and more power in all sorts of institutions. They need to ensure that working people feel more and more that it is their *right* to control larger and larger elements of society and to fashion these elements under their democratic control. Thus we would judge struggles as being revolutionary or reformist *not* simply around the content of the policy being struggled over, but the way in which that policy will be controlled. This can be exemplified by looking at the struggles against the public expenditure cuts. Simply to defend the extent and form of the service as it is at present carried out is an important reformist struggle; it can be one that becomes a part of the revolutionary process if it provides experiences which promote more power for working people in actually controlling the form and nature of services; if it extends democracy into the very nature of welfare provision. This stress on democracy goes far beyond the forms of representative democracy which have shown to be such a weak vehicle of change for Labour governments and Labour councils. It is essential that representative democracy is challenged by direct democracy in terms of the day-to-day relationship of workers and clients to the state. To this end we will propose that the local state is a crucial political concept which defines both an area of struggle and the basis for the development of important political forces. The local state provides at one and the same time an experience of a *service provider*; an experience of *representative citizenship* through local elections; an experience of *cultural locality* (that is, an experience of life as a person from Leeds or Coventry). Those experiences form a crucial potential relationship since they cross over the boundaries of struggle within the state and struggles external to it. Those areas that have launched any really successful struggle against the cuts have included not only those that receive the service but those that work in it and the local representatives in, for instance, an area health authority or the local Labour council.

In the remainder of the book we hope to demonstrate that these political considerations about welfare can be used as a part of an analysis of welfare work and partly as a prescription for welfare work and politics. In this process we would underline the necessity for the progressive and flexible use of marxist theory in its relationship to work and struggle.

2
Welfare Workers and the Changing British State

Our ideas are directed primarily at welfare workers within the British state in the 1980s. It is not to imply that welfare workers are in any obvious way *more* important than the people they work with and for, rather that they face a number of separate and different problems from other types of workers. This work is mainly directed at those differences; differences that we feel emerge precisely because we work for welfare aspects of the British state.

Before trying to elaborate upon the attempt at socialist practice within this work, we will open three major areas of analysis. We use the word 'open' deliberately, because much of the left's analysis so far has been one that closes off the development of ideas — a closure that hinders any attempts at socialist practice by crudely linking state welfare work with phrases like 'social control'. We feel that the closure of these ideas has happened primarily because of a traditional 'subordinate' consciousness on the left. We will use the word 'subordinate' a great deal in describing left politics in Britain, because we feel it reflects the traditional experience that revolutionary socialists have in this country. 'Subordinate' because their ideas and politics have had to contend with being marginal to the mainstream of political struggle. This has caused us to see ourselves as an opposition, and, inevitably, a minority opposition to developments in welfare. Any attempt to involve oneself openly with the construction of policy within the welfare field, as we trust this book will show, runs the risk of being branded 'class collaborationist' or 'selling out'. We feel that it is necessary for socialists within welfare to take seriously the opportunities for the formulation and the implementation of policy *within* that capitalist state. But to do that, we would suggest, it is necessary to shrug off this subordinate consciousness. Such a 'shrugging off' is not a simple, idealistic act; rather, it takes an *involvement* in political discussions and action that can only be experienced fully in the construction of socialism itself. We will return to this vital process later, as we examine a number of practice examples.

First, we will show the way in which all of the major changes in central and local government organisations within which people work have been linked to an overall change in the form of the government of the state. This process we will call 'restructuring of the state apparatus'. We all know that there have been numerous changes in the structure of welfare work, yet few of us in our daily lives experience the true breadth of these changes. As a consequence, we see them all as *discrete*, as separate changes within *this or that organisation*. Our analysis will show how all of these changes are directly linked to the economic and political problems faced by British capitalism. What we hope to demonstrate is that these alterations, put forward as neutral changes in government administration, are in fact only one form of political change — and a form that meets the needs of only a tiny section of the population of Britain.

Second, we want to underline the fact that it is not *only* change in welfare organisations that has occurred. Even more importantly the overall life of all working people has been 'restructured' over the period from 1962 to the present day. This is sometimes experienced as 'the end of community', or 'the breakdown of moral fibre', or, more weakly, 'the pace of change', 'the country going to the dogs'. Such common-sense views of these changes actually signal what have been massive changes constructed by the political and economic problems faced by British capitalism. Therefore, *both* the changes in government, *and* the changes in working-class lives have the same set of causes.

This brings us to our third area of analysis — the relationship between these changed welfare apparatuses and the changed lives of working people. Since most welfare state work is with working-class people, it is *this* relationship that,

in many ways, constructs both the main aim of the restructured state, *and* the way in which socialists must construct
their practice and politics around it. To give a concrete
example of this new relationship: a welfare assistant has to
cope with the redundancy and housing problems of a single
mother in an area social services office. Now, of course it is
true that unemployment, bad housing, single parenthood and
social services existed before, but the recent changes in all of
these elements and organisations have been massive and, we
believe, indissolubly linked. Similarly, it is only by attempting
politically to transform the relationship between that state
worker and client that any real improvement in welfare can
be achieved.

HOW DO WE UNDERSTAND THE RESTRUCTURING OF
WELFARE ORGANISATIONS?

In the first chapter of the book we discussed the different
ways of understanding the British welfare state. It is vitally
important for the reader to understand that, contrary to
popular belief, a 'marxist' analysis contains many disagreements. Historically there have been those — and indeed, there
still are — who believe that there is one 'true' marxism, and
all other variants are to be completely dismissed. Rather, we
believe that marxism is a method of understanding the world
which does lead to many different marxisms. These differences
always have a theoretical and a political significance, and in
Chapter 1 we explained what some of these theoretical
disagreements mean in relation to our own position. Later on
in the book we will describe the way in which our analysis
provides a different practice and politics for state workers.
Here, however, we wish to make sense of this in relation to
the changing structure of government organisations in the
United Kingdom and the resulting change in the working
conditions of welfare workers.

There have been two significant ways of making sense of
the major changes in state apparatus. The first of these is the
dominant way of making sense of the world of politics, and
it is crucial to our whole argument. It is called social democ-

racy, and we have looked at its major themes already. Within this perspective the many changes that have occurred within government departments are seen as aiming simply to increase the efficiency of these organisations. Thus, new boundaries, new structures of organisations, new forms of a more rational service, new ways of saving money and of redefining 'needs', are all seen as coming from a simple process of improvement. This process is, by and large, a neutral one which is non-political. Within this approach politics is primarily about the 'content' of the organisation, the 'content' of, for example, a school's curriculum; the extent of benefit, say, within social security; but in both cases the nature of the organisation, its *form*, is seen to be non-political. We will argue forcibly against this analysis, indeed, we see these changes as deeply political: we feel welfare workers experience these organisational forms as directly constraining their work, and that this constraint affects the way in which they can provide services. Such things are not only political, but also, as we will demonstrate, directly linked with on another.

As a direct alternative to this social democratic framework, others have seen these changes as a part of a wider political process. The changes in state organisation are seen as part of a ruling class strategy, and these writers provide an invaluable breakthrough in so far as they highlight clearly areas of change that had previously been ignored by the marxist left: parts of political life that had literally been a section of the backdrop were thrown into the centre of the stage. Thus, John Benington emphasises that the form of organisation within local government, 'corporate management', was itself deeply affecting the tone of political decisions make by local councillors. Similarly, Cynthia Cockburn (1977) shows the way in which the development of corporate management was attended by a community strategy reaching out into the locality.

These writers changed the way in which many of us thought about the organisations within which we worked. However, we have important disagreements with them because, while it is true that they put these administrative changes into the arena of politics, at every stage they seem to paint a picture of these political changes as being totally run by the ruling class. What this class wants to achieve, it achieves. We feel that they underplay the role of the working class in this whole process; presenting a very unilinear view of the way in which change occurs. We see such an analysis as one kind of marxism — we want to stress another.

Our marxism will underline the role of the working class in the daily restructuring of capitalism, and *therefore* will stress the possibilities for state workers in engaging directly in this politics. Such a political involvement would entail state welfare workers having to link closely with other working-class organisations in order to fight for a different form of welfare — a welfare that we feel would represent a real platform for a transformation to socialism. Politically this position poses the possibility of involving the mass of working people in the struggle for socialism within, and against, the contradictions that exist in the capitalist system. It sees that certain victories within capitalism are victories for the political economy of the working class, as against the ruling class. This was how Marx saw the Factory Acts of the 1840s: a victory that we feel is repeated over the following century, but is rarely consolidated because of the political failures of the working class itself. We see the struggles that took place in the 1970s around welfare provision as being struggles between working-class organisations and their opponents. In order to demonstrate this theory and politics we will deal with the overall change in the British state in four major sections: first, why it was necessary for British capitalism to change in the 1960s and 1970s; second, how did the particularities of the political ideas and structures of the British working class affect the state and economic policies; third, why did the state intervene in the way it did in the lives of working-class people; and finally, why was it necessary to restructure the state itself as an integral part of this process, and what does this mean for welfare workers?

We feel that this contemporary history of change is important for welfare workers to know and understand. With the important exception of Hall *et al.* (1978), very little accessible contemporary history is written for practitioners, and as such, we feel that some political activity is ill informed.

WHAT WAS HAPPENING TO BRITISH CAPITAL IN 1962?

Before we begin to answer this question, we must make two points for welfare workers. First, that the 'economy' of the United Kingdom is one that can only be understood by comprehending the conflicting problems of two different classes. As we will show, it is nonsense to suggest that the 'economy' suffers problems; rather, certain problems are suffered by those who own the major parts of the private economy, and certain problems are experienced by those who work for their living. Such a distinction between classes is basic to marxism (q.v. Hunt, 1977), yet it needs to be explained in contemporary terms when we carry out recent historical analysis. For over the last fifteen years we have lived in a society where there has been a perpetual crisis within the 'economy'; where the 'economy' takes on a life of its own with its own illnesses and its own cures. Similarly, the 'national interest' with its 'ailing pound' has been introduced as a value-free notion. As Hall *et al.* (1978) have cleafly noted:

> Between 1972 and the present as the 'national interest' has become unequivocally identified with whatever policies the state is currently pursuing, the reality of the state has come to provide the raison d'etre for the media: once any group threatening this delicately poised strategy has been symbolically cast out of the body politic — through the mechanisms of the moderate/extremist paradigm — the media have felt it quite legitimate to intervene. (Hall *et al.*, 1978, p. 307)

Throughout our work we will explore the economic problems as problems for owners, capitalists, for the bourgeoisie, *or* problems for workers and their children.

Secondly, we must establish the importance of these economic relations for welfare workers. Since 1975 we have all come to realise the effect of 'public expenditure cuts' upon the very possibility of welfare within our work; we have learnt to gauge the power of economic relationships in everything from housing policy through zimmer frames to the amount of time and energy we need to talk to a child before he or she comes before juvenile court. However, here we want to explore this relationship at a much deeper level; a level that demonstrates the effect of the economic problems for capital as something that structures the very administrational service of our welfare work. We think that the area of wages and profit, an area that has dominated the media politics of the last fifteen years, has not been something separate from the world of welfare.

What then were the problems facing capital in Britain in 1962? At an economic level the 'crisis' cannot simply be said to have started in 1962. The collapse of the British Empire ended a series of cheap and exploitable markets both for raw materials and for finished products. These markets, secured by armed force, had prevented the collapse of British industrial infrastructure. As Eric Hobsbawm lucidly explains (1965) British capitalism was hampered again and again by its position as the first industrialised capitalist economy. Even the Empire could not hide this forced degeneration of the industrial base. By the 1960s, though, the historic weakness was there for all to see. This became especially true when the British economy was compared to 'foreign competitors'. It was at this stage that capital most comprehensively began to find other forms and other areas of exploitation in other countries. It became obvious that the industrial base of the United Kingdom was expendable to capitalism but only at the cost of intense social disruption to the people who happened to live here. Table 1 shows the slowing down of growth rate in the gross national product in the late 1950s and early 1960s. The figures are not over-dramatic; for example, a similar table of the 1970s would show an actual drop in production. However, in a world capitalist economy that was growing much, much quicker, this slow growth rate was the factor that signified a

TABLE 1 Growth in *GNP*

	1957	1958	1959	1960	1961	1962
£000	20 068	20 030	20 644	21 558	21 558	22 186

TABLE 2 Amount of GNP going to varied sources

	Factor income GNP	Money from employment	Gross trading profits
1957	19 118	12 926	3 120
1958	19 720	13 223	3 017
1959	20 912	14 044	3 336
1960	22 675	15 090	3 685
1961	23 864	16 275	3 487
1962	24 774	17 009	3 474

much greater problem. It was itself the cause of a future problem in that it signalled not only a slow growth rate, but also proved that the country could not generate sufficient wealth to invest in its future.

This slow growth rate hid other crucial changes within the different proportions of the economy that went to wages and profits. Table 2 shows these proportions and makes the point that over six years profits increased by £300 million. In fact, this was a drop in the percentage of the gross national product, from 16 per cent to 14 per cent. Such a fall creates difficulties for capital, but it is not dramatic, since it simply has to drop the amount that it invests for a small period. Yet, if we look at Table 3, we see that gross capital formation within the United Kingdom increased by £500 million. This means that, at this time, it was necessary to invest even more in plant in

TABLE 3 Gross capital formation

	Total	Public sector	Private sector
1957	3 376	1 159	1 600
1958	3 493	1 205	1 697
1959	3 722	1 312	1 752
1960	4 107	1 385	1 968
1961	4 570	1 517	2 232
1962	4 626	1 633	2 120

the United Kingdom, yet there was actually a smaller amount to invest. What does this mean? It means that it was necessary in a competing capitalist economy to increase the size of capital holdings in order to re-tool, actually to invest *more and more*. Yet the amount of profit being produced in the 1960s was not growing fast enough for this to happen. This meant that capital was not extracting sufficient profit within the United Kingdom to ensure its future ability to reproduce itself. This problem was compounded by the necessity to invest more and more, as technology changed the process of production.

However, as we shall see, all such discussions about 'profitability' and 'British capital' are rather limited in so far as the actual choices made by boards of directors about investments have never been bounded by the limits of the United Kingdom. One of the crucial aspects of capital is that much of it can be shifted about the world to a place where it can be used to exploit people to greater effect. Consequently, in the 1880s, British capital had gone to the expanding Empire, and had been directly controlled not only by British boards of directors, but also by British state institutions. In the 1960s and 1970s we see a similar flow of capital abroad, and the evacuation of the traditional industrial base of the British economy. As we shall see, this is accompanied by the growth of merchant and other banks as dominant institutions. When capital takes the form of finance it can be shifted about the world most easily; when in the form of machines it proves more difficult. What is crucial to underline is that the multinational finance company feels no direct cultural or political involvement with the cities, towns and regions it abandons. It operates to its own logic. There is no reason internal to that logic to expect anything very different.

There were other factors within the world economy that directly affected this history. We see the rise to eventual dominance of 'foreign competition' within several sectors of the British economy. As the Board of Trade notes, 'From 1951—1961 production in the textile sectors of industry fell by 7% though output in productive industries rose by 33% (HMSO, 1962a, p. 3427). Exports of textiles from Great Britain fell by 24 per cent from 1954—61. Yet *world* exports of textiles rose by 25 per cent of the same period. Thus the base for the U.K. export industry within the world market was crumbling. (It is interesting to note that this Board of Trade report only *notes* this process, and gives little assistance or advice, except to call for more *energy* in searching out markets. The tone of this report contrasts sharply with the hectoring tone of later government reports when the state begins to take a very direct hand in restructuring the economy, and tends to influence capital movement much more.) Apart from textiles, if we look at the orders in hand for the engineering industry over this period (Table 4), we see a slowing down in orders and a drop in the year 1961–2. Or rather, the changes show that capital's interest in the industrial base of the United Kingdom could only be maintained by a massive increase in investment, and, as we shall see, this means that capital evacuates this traditional base in favour of new profits and new forms.

TABLE 4 Orders in hand for engineering industry base 1958

1958	1959	1960	1961 1st qtr	1961 2nd qtr	1961 3rd qtr	1961 4th qtr	1962 1st qtr	1962 2nd qtr	1962 3rd qtr
100	101	117	127	126	124	120	121	120	119

Source   HMSO, *Gazette*, 1962, p. 1061

Table 4 shows the specific nature of what was happening at this moment, to this sector of capital. Similarly, if we look at the growth of exports in manufacturing industry by main exporting counties over the period 1954–61 we see the slow rate of growth of the United Kingdom as against the rest.

The figures in Table 5 underline the powerful growth of the rest of the capitalist world's manufacturing economies in comparison to that of the United Kingdom. Of course, with hindsight, we can see the real depth of the collpase that was beginning to occur then. The intervening years have measured the continued decline of British industrial capitalism; what is significant about this period is that it marked the stage when

TABLE 5   Exports of manufacturing by main exporting companies,
1954—61 (% *growth in each country over the period*)

UK	EEC	Sweden	Switzerland	USA	Canada	Japan	Total
45	127	121	68	50	39	171	85

the government first really noticed this process; it also marked
the stage when British capital started to do something about
it.

WHAT DOES CAPITAL DO IN THIS SITUATION?

In the face of this problem, British capital begins to change
the face and structure of British industry. One of the major
processes involved is popularly known as the 'take-over'. The
weaker capitalist firms are swallowed up by their competitors
creating even stronger and stronger units of production. The
process was noted by the Board of Trade at an early juncture:

> There was an increase in business concentration during the
> three years (1958—60). The largest one hundred companies
> at the end of 1957 already accounted for 51% of total net
> assets of quoted companies and by the end of 1960 the
> share of these one hundred largest companies has risen to
> 54% . . . Typical companies to show a high rate of expan-
> sion in net assets were large companies earning a high rate
> of return on capital, but depending on the capital market
> for a high proportion of the finance on the used in expan-
> sion. (BOT, *Finance and growth of U.K. companies,*
> *1958—60*)

Only the large organisation could effectively provide sufficient
profits to continue in competition. Consequently, larger
firms increasingly took over the ailing smaller firms, and it
was the larger firms that increased their assets. In Table 6 we
can see that, of the firms with assets over £25 millions, over
two thirds grew by 20 per cent; whereas, of the firms with

TABLE 6 Growth of net assets 1958—60 by size of company

Size of company by net assets	% increase in net assets		
£000	20	10—19	10
25 000+	68	18	14
10 000—25 000	65	19	16
5 000—10 000	54	24	22
2 500—5 000	50	25	25
500 — 2 500	43	28	29
100—500	43	24	34
100	34	22	44
Total	43	24	33

less than £1 000 000 assets, only one third grew by the same proportion.

Thus by itself capital began to cope with the worst of its problems of low profitability. It coped by increasing its size and merging into different industries. However, these *internal* changes to the nature of capitalist enterprises do not simply change the names of firms, or the size of their buildings. They actually mean a series of enormous changes in the nature of the work of those employed in these firms. There are three effects of great significance for these employees. First, it meant changes in the people who own the factories, involving smaller units as a part of much larger firms. Consequently, those who made the real decisions controlling the lives of the workforce receded further and further from that workforce. This meant that there is less and less chance for that work-force to be able to affect their decisions directly. It meant that the board of directors were able to make decisions to close down factories that, in terms of the whole firm, were only a minor fraction; but, in terms of the towns and cities where these factories existed, often totally changed the economy of a town.

Secondly, these larger units were formed primarily to *rationalise* the process of production. What does this phrase mean? In terms of the people working in the factories it means many different changes in the way in which they work. It means that these changes occur at an ever-increasing pace: each change following even harder on the heels of the last. Given the distance of the decision-makers from this process one minor decision taken at the bottom of an agenda can change the experience of work for tens of thousands of workers, with no real reference to them at all. Rationalisation at its boldest is quite simply sacking sections of the workforce when the work in firm C, which has just been taken over by multinational A, is no longer required by the new owners, because they have workers elsewhere in their firm doing those jobs. Therefore, rationalisation often lead to redundancies.

These then are the *direct* repercussions of the changes in capital. On a day-to-day basis this necessary restructuring of industry in the interests of capital produces a major change in the work lives of millions of people. More drastically, it throws many thousands of workers out of a job when their factory goes through the 'rationalising' process. However, this form of being 'rational' is *dominated* by one logic only, and that is the logic of capital. This logic does not itself take the day-to-day effects upon human beings into account; indeed, such humanity operates as an opposing force to the logic of capitalist restructuring and it is alongside that opposition that this book places itself.

Over the past eighteen years, though, politicians, government officers and media experts have nearly all worked within the logic of capitalist restructuring as the *only* way out of the crisis of British capitalism. Many of them have been genuinely concerned with the plight of unemployed workers, or workers whose lives have been turned inside out by this 'logic'; others of them genuinely care very little. Both groups, however, are united in the belief that there is simply no alternative to these 'difficult' changes.

However the changes that have occurred have not *simply* been worked out by capital against labour. Over the past 100 years, since the granting of the vote, the working class have helped to construct a series of institutions which stop capital from running, or from changing, society *simply* in its own image. The Labour Party, the trade union movement, all operate in the last resort *within* that logic of capital. But they also try to operate in such a way as to interpret that logic, as far as possible, in the interests of the working people.

Consequently, when the state becomes involved in this restructuring process, it is here that the direct effect of the working class is felt in the overall project. It is here that a number of complex political relationships occur; and since we will contend that it is these political relationships that dominate our lives as welfare workers in the 1970s and 1980s, it is essential to explore fully the way in which the state relates to the economic problems outlined above.

We will explain that the state plays three roles in this process of restructuring. First, it actually assists in the restructuring of capital itself. Secondly, it assists in the way in which labour is changed to fit in with the new needs of capital. Here we are approaching some of the major areas in the work of state welfare workers. Thirdly, the state itself is restructured to carry out its own work more easily in areas one and two. Importantly, all of these activities are, by and large, carried out in a social democratic way. Thus capital is assisted; the state is changed; and the position of ordinary men and women as workers is changed, in a social democratic form. Therefore, we will start by further elaborating upon exactly what social democracy means in this context.

SOCIAL DEMOCRACY – MAKING THE BEST OF AN IMPOSSIBLE JOB

The sub-title refers to the fact that social democracy as an ideology is adhered to by millions of working-class people as the best way they can extract policy in their favour in this society. We would contend that, for most of this period, the ideology of social democracy is the one adhered to not only by the working class but also by the state and the legislature. It is the dominant ideology of post-war Britain. If it is generally dominant it specifically holds an almost mono-polistic position within the welfare state.

Given that we see the restructuring of capital and therefore labour as occurring within this ideology, it is obviously a vital one to explore. But first, and crucially, what do we mean when we say that all these changes took place *within* an ideology? Really, such a phrase tries to describe the import- ance we attach to ideology, for the reality of ideology goes far beyond ideas. For our purposes ideology is also about institutions, about the way in which they actually imbue and reproduce an ideology in their structure, their form, and on occasion in their bricks and mortar. Thus, to take a welfare example, the workhouse represented an ideology contained in its procedures, its buildings and its social relationships; the means test represents a variant of that ideology. The poor must be and feel *punished*. Therefore when we say that a set of institutions have been restructured and changed within an ideology, we are giving that ideology a great deal of import- ance. As we shall try to show, that ideology has been created by a whole set of class struggles within the United Kingdom over the last 150 years, and does not merely consist of a few speeches or ideas. In Chapter 1 we tried to outline the different ideologies that exist within the welfare state. Here we are underlining their importance by pointing out that institutions within which we work are constructed *by* ideologies, and then these institutions themselves *reproduce* ideologies. As the book unfolds, we will give specific examples of this process.

HOW DOES SOCIAL DEMOCRACY RELATE TO THE CHANGES IN THE WORKING CLASS AND IN THE ECONOMY?

So far, we have made out a case for the economic necessity of capital restructuring itself, and the labour force, alongside the restructuring of all aspects of the state. We have also argued that the dominant set of political ideas that effected this was social democracy, a set of ideas that had some real, daily influence upon working people. It is now necessary to understand how the specific politics of social democracy actually play a part in that process. We are explaining this in order to try to stress the important idea that the structure of the welfare state and the organisation of welfare work within it are deeply political and highly constructed: we are underlining the fact that, if once constructed one way, they can be reconstructed in another. Such a lesson is vital if we, as welfare workers and socialists, are to play a role in changing the politics of the state.

One of the major institutions that has been responsible for linking social democracy with the restructuring of welfare, has been the Labour Party. The important fact about the Labour Party for this analysis is that it straddles both working-class politics *and* state policy — in other words, it actually represents the political ideas and aspirations of millions of people, while simultaneously developing elements of social policy and 'governing' state structures. The revolutionary left has found this a difficult truth to come to terms with since it emphasises their own lack of power. However, while we may all wish the working class to move further towards the left, for much of this century the Labour Party has represented — not exactly, but largely — the political consciousness of working people.

Thus social democracy has represented working-class interests in so far as they are articulated in a mass way. However in representing those interests through state policy, Labour governments and councils have frequently failed. On the whole, since social democracy sees the interests of working people as being represented *within* a capitalist society, it is not surprising that it is in *this* form that those interests are reflected at a level of state policy. Thus, there is an organic relationship within the United Kingdom between the hopes and aspirations of working people, and those, primarily Labour Party politicians, who have created state welfare policy — but this organic relationship exists *within* the dominance of capitalist social relationships. This means that such dominant relationships as the profit motive, interest rates, private property or individualism, still exert their dominant interest in the development of social policy. Consequently, taken in total, social democracy represents a set of ideas that are directly, and necessarily, *contradictory in both form and content.* They represent partially the interests of both capitalists and the working class, and will therefore *always* be essentially unstable.

Social democracy then has two important elements: first, it represents the clear link in the United Kingdom between state power and the working class; second, it contains inevitable contradictions since it tries to operate for that class within a capitalist society. If it were not an *organic* link, then its importance would be greatly diminished, and if it were *not* contradictory then it could be simply accepted as working class or dismissed as ruling class.

This, then, is the crux of our analysis. Social democracy contains inevitable contradictions within it. *It is itself an arena of class struggle.* Any social democratic policies can, to some extent, represent the interests of the working class, or, the interests of the capitalist class; these interests conflict within both the construction and the implementation of these policies. The way in which they actually evolve and are put into practice is wholly affected by the nature and structure of the class struggle in our society. Since we are a part of that class struggle, we can play an active role in it as state workers.

The process of restructuring is one that fits within this theory: social democracy, since it took capitalist society as its starting and finishing point, *had* to operate a policy of restructuring. Yet, since it was social democracy, it was affected by the interests of working people. This process inevitably contains contradictions through which welfare workers can play a part. How they can do this we shall see later.

WHAT PART DOES THE LABOUR PARTY PLAY?

Might it not be more useful to see the Labour party as . . . a party which itself reflects the struggle between the dominant and subordinate classes. Also, would it not be fruitful to see it as a party divided by the lines of this struggle, and uniquely enjoying the confidence of both sides. (How else could Labour Governments work?) It embodies, that is, the given compromise which has been established between the hegemonic and subordinate class. Ought not the starting point of an analysis of the Labour party be found in the particular strength of reformism, the frailty of the Communist Party, and the weakness of a marxist tradition? All these can be logically connected. (Robinson, 1978)

While we start from the premise that the Labour Party of itself cannot construct a revolutionary working class in this country, we argue that both as a political party and as a part of a government it will have a vital role to play. Thus, we do not have to show in this work that the Labour Party is not a revolutionary socialist party; rather, we have to show that it has potential for the working class, and for progressive forces — a potential greater than is now being achieved; we need to show that, for welfare workers, the major social democratic party and the role it plays in relation to 'welfare' is vitally important.

One of the crucial distinctions that we will continually draw, is the relationship between form and content in welfare policy. Most of the analyses put forward by the Labour Party centre around the content of their proposed policies — whether these policies are 'socialist', 'reformist' or 'reactionary'. Here, we do not wish to enter into that particular discussion, but rather to point out that the form of the Labour Party plays a crucial role in the way it relates to the state.

Within the sphere of central government, the Labour Party has several points of contact: first, it stands in elections, and it sees the results of those elections in terms of 'winning' state power. However, when it 'wins' state power, it also hands over that power to a separate group within the party, the parliamentary Labour Party. The conference itself has no jurisdiction over the votes of the Labour members, because the Labour Party accords with the doctrine of parliamentary sovereignty — a doctrine that gives Members of Parliament the right to vote as they wish, unless subject to the whip of the parliamentary party, which is decided in Cabinet (or in the shadow Cabinet).

This structure also holds true for local councils, where local councillors have a triple relationship: one with the party, another with their 'wards', and a third with the leaders of the Labour group (the most important one). Such a structure means that we must see the Labour Party as a contradictory political structure, yet still one that has mass political support. Thus it has been through the Labour Party that a great deal of the restructuring of the state apparatuses has taken place. Much of the community strategy, much of the children's legislation and the organisation of social services, has occurred under Labour governments and through Labour Party policies.

Consequently, when we talk about social democratic politics in the UK we have to discuss the effect of Labour governments on state policy and on working people. Historically this is discussed admirably in Gough (1979) and Ginsburg (1979); what concerns us here is the need to characterise some of the major elements of the state form that Labour governments have created in the periods 1945—51 and 1964—70. Our interest is with the second period and we will concentrate on the themes that emerge during this period.

HOW DOES THE LABOUR PARTY/SOCIAL DEMOCRACY RESTRUCTURE THE STATE?

We have suggested that the Labour Party and social democracy see the state as the crucial element of change in a capitalist society. The state is the institution which 'nationalises the commanding heights' of industry; the state is the organisation which stops the excesses of capitalism. Yet, as we have suggested, the Labour Party has little theoretical or practical idea of the state and how it relates to capitalism; or how it relates to working people. Nearly all of the restructuring of the state that has taken place in the 1960s and 1970s has reflected the belief that the changes were a neutral rationalisation of a system that had simply 'got out of date' or had 'got confused by extra powers'. Thus the first theme that emerges is the view that all the changes are in the nature of an administrative reorganisation and not something that involves a political movement.

Secondly, and linked to this 'statism', is the movement towards bigger and more centralised authorities. This applies not only to the larger local authorities but also to changes in police authorities, water authorities, gas authorities, and so on. It is assumed within this element of social democracy that only large, powerful state organisations have the strength to take on and regulate monopoly capital. Equally since these organisations will be controlled by Labour politicians the stronger they are then the stronger will be the labour movement.

Thirdly, bigger and improved state authorities are linked, by social democrats, to the idea of progress. This represents a very important theme in this book. There are many occasions when Labour politicians have attacked trade unionists for being Luddites when they have tried to defend their jobs; have attacked community organisations for being reactionary when they are trying to defend their homes; have attacked residents' associations as being narrow minded when they have tried to stop a road-building scheme in their community. Size, and the large view of things, have been inextricably linked with progress for social democracy and locality has been linked with small-minded factionalism.

This attitude was of particular importance in the 1964 election and in the whole philosophy and election slogans of the Labour Party over the period. Wilson coined a particularly telling phrase which is worth expanding. The white hot heat of the technological revolution was going to forge Britain's future and he was clear what would happen to those who stood in the way.

Mr. Chairman, let me conclude with what I think the message of all this is for Conference . . . we are redefining and we are restating our Socialism in terms of scientific revolution. But that revolution cannot become a reality unless we are prepared to make far-reaching changes in economic and social attitudes which permeate our whole system of society. The Britain that is going to be forged in the white heat of this revolution will be no place for restrictive practices or for out-dated methods on either side of industry. (Labour Party, 1963)

This statement had implications that went far beyond industry and into the way in which the state was organised. Size, administrative tidiness and progress, all part of the centralisation of the state apparatuses, are given a great deal of attention within social democratic argument and policy.

Fourthly, the process of restructuring was one that put its faith in expertise. In part this was another political reaction against the faded amateurism that seemed to characterise the past in British life and found its true apparent champion in Sir Alec Douglas-Home. But it also reflected a belief in experts as the promoters of progress, and as the only people capable of carrying out their expertise in a politically neutral way. Though this was especially true in the case of the restructuring of the welfare state, a similar case could be made out for the changes in industrial policy constructed by successive Labour governments (Fryer and Martin, 1971). This belief in 'experts' is grounded in Labour Party thinking, as an examination of the history of the Labour Party in relation to welfare will show.

Starting with the Webbs (Abrams, 1965) and their relationship with the Labour Party's policy on the Poor Law in the first decade of the century, the Labour Party, as a party with a relationship to the working class and on occasions a large membership, has failed to involve that membership or that class in the day-to-day construction of social policies. One of the best examples was the Labour Party's policy on social security between 1939 and the present day. First, following Lord Beveridge (who was after all a *Liberal* Lord) and then in the wake of Richard Titmuss's rewriting of the National Superannuation Scheme in the 1950s, the policy of the Labour Party was not merely affected by the opinions of experts — it was *written* by them. On occasions of course these experts were indeed members of the Labour Party and were therefore a 'part of the movement'. But they represented a very elite part of that movement; not one that had a close relationship with, for example, the trade union movement.

However we are talking here about not just the content of policy, which was written by experts, but the implementation of those policies within state structures. Thus, the structures that were created by social democracy over this period gave greater practical power to experts. The most notable example was that of corporate management (Cockburn, 1977) where Labour authority after Labour authority constructed a system of government which in practical terms has taken even more power away from elected members.

Politically, it is only in recent years that the Labour Party, or rather sections of it, have realised the *political* power of 'experts' and civil servants. Richard Crossman's diaries demonstrate time and again how the civil servants and the experts in various ministries were *not* simply at his beck and call to carry out policy. It is a disturbing reflection on the lack of political thinking in the Labour leadership that Crossman, whilst suffering from the effects of this process, was a party to the construction of state bodies that gave more and more practical power to 'experts and civil servants'. The Seebohm Report and the resulting Act of Parliament occurred during his tenure as minister.

THE RELATIONSHIP BETWEEN RESTRUCTURED STATE AND CAPITAL

So far we have constructed two prongs to our argument. First, we outlined the practical necessity for capital to restructure itself in the UK around larger and larger elements, with greater centralisation of power in fewer hands. We also argued that this would have massive and occasionally brutal effects upon the day-to-day lives of working people, both at work and at home. Secondly, we have argued that social democracy has been the major ideology that has 'governed' this restructuring of the state, promoting as it has a centralisation of power and a granting of more power to experts. We have also argued that the politics of social democracy are constructed around contradiction: although social democracy did give some thought to the problems of the working class caused by the restructuring of capital, it also carried out its policies within the logic of capital. It is to this last element, which in a way brings both arguments together, that we now want to turn.

In arguing that social democracy is contradictory we want to make two political points. First, that it is absurd to exclude the working class from any account of the restructuring process. The working class is a part of that process because social democracy — to a greater or lesser extent — takes their political, social and ideological reactions into account. However, social democracy *also* works within the boundaries of capitalist economic and social relations and therefore argued for a restructuring of the state and economy which was seen as absolutely essential. Thus the Labour government's arguments over the whole period have been that 'there was no alternative' to all these changes; there was no alternative to increasing profitability; to increasing job disruption; progress and profit were synonymous. Those that stood in the way were Luddites. As much as possible would be done to soften the effects upon the working class but capital, labour and the state *had* to be restructured.

Much of the rest of this book explores some of the specifics of that process and we conclude with a political discussion of alternatives. But first it is necessary to explain some of the effect of this upon welfare workers, since they have a dual relationship with the process: they work within the organisations we have been discussing, and they nearly all agree with social democratic politics. Why is it that most welfare workers are social democrats? There are two major reasons for this. First, working within the welfare state one has a basic interest in an ideology which grants power and progress to welfare state institutions. Their collapse or their lack of importance means that welfare workers will be out of a job. Secondly, and less out of self-interest, welfare workers tend to pick jobs in welfare because they are predisposed to agree with the role of welfare in helping people to deal with particular crises in their lives.

Both of these aspects mean that welfare workers are tied up with the future of welfare. The restructuring that has occurred in all these apparatuses has been represented as being in the best interests of welfare. Nearly all of these changes were put forward as strengthening welfare against the capitalist ethics of the market. Consequently, with a number of specific exceptions concerned with special interest, these changes in the state were welcomed by welfare workers. For one reason, as we have seen, they seemed to give greater responsibility and power to the experts. In this context the experts were the professionals in welfare.

RESTRUCTURING CAPITAL AND RESTRUCTURING PEOPLE'S LIVES

We started this chapter by discussing the power and importance of the economy for welfare workers; we have tried to show *how* the restructuring of capital forced a restructuring of the state apparatus. It is obvious that most welfare workers actually work *within* organisations that have been affected by these changes. However we want to conclude this analysis by underlining the fact that the aim of all these changes was to affect the lives of working people. The purpose was to change the places in which they live, to move them around until they fit in with the new and restructured needs of capital. These changes, like the changes in state structure, may start with the place of work, the point of production, but they inevitably include the rest of a person's life.

> More rapid industrial and technological change will be required to achieve a faster rate of economic growth. This will involve movements of work people from declining industries to expanding industries, from less productive firms to more productive firms. To some extent movements of this kind are always going on and since the end of the war there have been substantial movements of workers between and within industries. Nevertheless if the necessary development is to be carried out smoothly and to the best advantage, measures will have to be taken to facilitate mobility of labour and to avoid the hardship of redundancy. These measures will involve the provision of housing accommodation increased transfer and resettlement allowances, better training facilities for displaced workers and better financial provision to tide over the redundant worker during the period he is unemployed. Unless these measures are taken, the fear of redundancy will make workers oppose change and employers will be less willing to release unnecessary labour for employment elsewhere. (HMSO, 1963, para 39)

In a way this is obvious; but most welfare workers in their day-to-day relationships with clients can easily forget the way in which people's lives have been transformed by the changes in the economy over the recent period. We want to underline this and also to point out that state policy has been fully aware of the necessary relationship between restructuring

capital, labour mobility and the home and community lives
of people. As the report continues

> The Committee of Inquiry into the Scottish Economy
> [Toothill Committee] concluded that while a wide variety
> of factors — family ties, custom, schools, communication,
> job opportunities, relative earnings — effect geographical
> mobility of labour, the most important factor is housing.
> Confirmation of this view has been provided in discussion
> with industries which have experiences of the problems of
> persuading workers to move to jobs in other areas. (HMSO,
> 1960, para 42)

The seventeen years between the publication of this report
and 1980 have seen a variety of different forms of state
policy aimed at encouraging labour mobility. Nearly all of
them have had a direct effect upon the lives of people in the
locality, as we shall see most clearly in Chapter 5. Here we
have tried simply to underline the real relationship between
economic crisis, state social democratic policy and people's
lives.

The next three chapters look specifically at team-based
social work, at child care and at community work in order to
explore the impact of state social democratic restructuring on
the lives of welfare workers and ordinary people. In each
chapter the contradictory effects of social democracy are
outlined and a mode of working with these contradictions is
discussed.

3

Seebohm – the Struggle for Collective Social Work

The present structure of British state welfare work was established by the reorganisation following the Local Authority Social Services Act by 1970. The Act received the Royal Assent on 29 May 1970 – the last day of the Labour-dominated Parliament, three weeks before Labour's election defeat and the return of the Heath government.

All marxist students of contemporary history will be aware that Acts of Parliament are not *caused* by government committees. The wastepaper baskets of Whitehall are littered with the reports of many committees set up by governments to hinder any reform. Whilst government committees have no legislative power themselves, their reports do represent crucial ideological documents. Therefore we must analyse the Seebohm Report, and the change in law that followed it.

The Committee was appointed towards the end of 1965 and briefed to 'review the organisation and responsibilities of the local authority personal social services in England and Wales, and to consider what changes are desirable to secure an effective family service'. The Committee was chaired by Sir Frederic Seebohm, chairman of Barclays Bank DCO and a director of Barclays Bank Limited. Apart from these limited qualifications as a state welfare worker, he had an active interest in voluntary social service, being particularly involved with Family Service Units and the National Council of Social Service. His major qualification, one that has a long pedigree in British ruling-class ideology, was that he was not over-identified with any of the state services that had a vested interest in the form of reorganisation. It is in this absurdly limited sense that this banker can be seen as an impartial

chairman; the qualification so beloved of British state circles
of the gifted amateur that forces a leading finance capitalist
to be selected as chairperson of a committee to reorganise
personal social services. It should be remembered of course
that he was selected by a Labour Cabinet.

Similarly the Committee membership was chosen so as not
to upset or exacerbate departmental rivalries. It consisted of
local government figures, three social work academics, a
medical figure, a representative of the voluntary sector, and
finally Lady James of Rusholme who had a wide range of
interests as a magistrate and voluntary worker.

Although we are not claiming that this membership alone
determined the tone and nature of the report it did have an
impact upon the text and the ideas contained within it.
Therefore the details of this membership are of some importance because of the glaring omissions in the committee roster.
We must not forget that they were all appointed by a Labour
government; yet the committee contained no trade union
representative; no representative of specifically working-class
organisations; no pressure groups; and no client groups. It is a
perfect example of social democratic politicians putting their
faith in 'experts' rather than in working-class organisations.
This is a point we will return to.

It is also noteworthy that women were poorly represented
(only two out of ten), despite the role that women play both
as providers of the service and as recipients of welfare
provision. Also, within the social work professions themselves,
there was strong representation of the establishment and no
rank and file social worker, nor was there anyone with detailed
recent knowledge in either the practice or receipt of the
service.

It is important to discuss the role of government committees
including Royal Commissions as a type of reform. This structure plays a crucial role in the story. In the previous chapter
we outlined the necessity for the reform of the state; we also
discussed the role of social democracy in the whole process.
It is within this form of analysis that we must look at this
particular government committee. One of the aspects of social
democracy which we noted is its preference for expertise
rather than the day-to-day experiences of working people;

similarly social democracy sees the state and the structure of the state as an enterprise that is above political debate, representing a neutral part of society.

It is therefore not surprising that a Labour government would not only select a government committee to construct the ideas of change but also that they would choose to people it with 'experts'. Put one way, a party that prides itself on representing the interests of working people then constructs a method of reform that is *distanced* enormously from working people. In terms of *either* day-to-day experience *or* organisational links there was no one on the Seebohm committee who related directly to the working class.

We do *not* see this as a simple 'sell out' by a Labour cabinet minister. Indeed, at the time there was very little debate either about choosing an alternative to a government committee, or about selecting a very different membership. There was no outburst from working people about these things; like the cabinet ministers, most working people accepted a social democratic view. They too felt that a government committee would come up with a 'fair' conclusion; that only clever experts would achieve that solution. Although we would strongly disagree with this abstracted form of change as a *socialist* form, we must recognise that in 1965, a viewpoint such as ours was a decidedly minority one. Instead the 1960s saw a virtual consensus on the progressive way forward, and it was a way that did not include, either in formulation or implementation, the involvement of working people themselves in welfare policy.

WHY IS THERE A DISTANCE BETWEEN WORKING PEOPLE AND PERSONAL SOCIAL SERVICE POLICY?

The attitude of the traditional institutions of the working class towards the personal social services has always been ambivalent. This ambivalence has sprung from the solid commitment of working people to social democracy as a force for change. This means that many trade unionists and activists argue for and defend the work of local authority social workers. They have seen such activity as a part of the state that provides help for the less fortunate, for the sick and the lame, the old and the weak. They are pleased that the state takes on these activities. They respect the power and importance of expertise in terms of the practitioners and the policy-makers; they also feel that such expertise makes for a neutral and non-political form of welfare practice.

On the other hand they also react very strongly against this 'professional' autonomy. It is seen as a way of putting the welfare worker above the 'ordinary person'; it creates a world where when someone actually comes into contact with a section of welfare provision they feel belittled by the 'expert'. Consequently there is a great deal of latent and increasingly explicit criticism of welfare 'know-alls who treat us like muck'.

We would stress that these two themes coexist, but that, by and large, the former side of the contradiction exists at the political level and the second at a more individualised level.

The politics of this particular book are aimed at overcoming this form of the relationship, which we see as invariably harmful, as inevitably leading to the weakening of progressive welfare politics, and a warped working-class consciousness. We are aiming along with many others to construct a much closer relationship between working-class organisations and progressive welfare workers' struggles. Much of this chapter is about certain concrete political events that have helped to provide a firm basis for this relationship; to construct alliances around issues in welfare that include working-class organisations.

These events and the resulting unity have taken place at different times and at different strengths throughout the country. Where it happens it forms a real base for the movement towards socialist practice. Consequently this chapter will spend some time looking not only at Seebohm but also at some examples of class struggle that local authority workers have been involved in. Such a stand is important since, by and large, the history of changes in the organisation of social services is a history in which working-class organisations have been conspicuous by their absence. Thus, whilst the first half of this chapter looks at the way in which the Seebohm reorganisation took place and how it fitted into the overall restructuring that occurred, we also look at some aspects of white-collar trade union organisation. We want to stress throughout this chapter that all these changes have been *constructed* and shaped around political imperatives. The message from this for welfare workers must be clear; that which has been shaped in one form can be *reshaped* and constructed in a different and more democratic form.

SEEBOHM AND SOCIAL DEMOCRACY

We have already asserted that the *form* and *content* of the Seebohm Committee was *par excellence* a social democratic form of change. Before looking at the particular recommendations contained in the Report and enacted in the present structure, we must outline the way in which we approach this analysis. Phoebe Hall (1976) provides a first class internal analysis of the report and the case for reform in terms of factors internal to the personal social services. Yet the important dynamics of the whole restructuring of the state and the economy that was going on around this particular reform is underplayed. So is a wider social and historical analysis.

We feel that it is essential not only to contextualise the Report in a general way, but to show the way in which the wider considerations that we outlined in Chapter 2 are carried out in the nuts and bolts of each reform. We feel this is especially important for practitioners, since an analysis which demonstrates that the reforms were purely *rational* dupes practioners into feeling that they themselves can simply bring about change by engaging in rational argument. Instead, constructing change is an activity that has to involve marshalling a large political coalition. It is important for us not to disarm progressive workers into seeing such change as easy.

It is equally important for us to analyse each aspect that we take up in terms of the wider politics of social democracy, to try to explain the dynamics of each of them as a part of social democratic politics. We do this not simply to discredit social democracy; rather, practitioners must be able to see the intricacies of their organisational structures as they are discussed in this chapter. They must then be able to relate to the wider historical understanding so that they may see *themselves* in history.

Indeed the Seebohm Report itself notes that they were reporting 'in a situation in which five bodies appointed by central government [the Plowden Council, the Maud and Mallaby Committees] are examining interrelated problems' (HMSO, 1968, para. 30). Importantly this interrelatedness of purpose was noted by the major Local Government Reform Committee, who noted that 'all personal social services, being closely linked in operation and effect, must be in the hands of one authority as strongly recommended by the recent report of the Seebohm Committee' (Redcliffe-Maud summary, para. 4).

In the previous chapter we tried to outline the interrelationships between all the different restructurings of the state in this period. We have tried to show the ways in which all these changes in the state were constructed within an economic and political problematic that was *at one and the same time* dominated by the power of monopoly capital but also had to recognise the power of a social democratic and organised working class. Within these wider political considerations we teased out the recurrent themes of all these changes. Within the Seebohm changes we will look at three of these: centralisation; area teams and community strategy; together with the importance of the reproduction of capitalist social relationships.

SEEBOHM AND CENTRALISATION

The central change brought about by the Seebohm Report was the creation of unified social service departments which would perform all the social service roles previously carried out by the children's, welfare, health, housing and education departments. Although in the final Act passed through Parliament the latter two were not included, the major reform following Seebohm was the creation of the single social service department with a single local authority committee responsible. This centralisation of responsibilities was explained very much in terms of the simplification of service delivery. Example after example was put forward of families who had social workers from several different departments rushing up their garden paths. This was, correctly, typified as chaotic both in terms of client experience and in terms of bureaucracy. Though here we must reiterate the point that of these two different concerns about the effects of chaos the bureaucrats were well represented on the Committee and the clients not at all. This must have meant that the client experience was reported to the Committee at least *third hand* and that the major concern was with the chaos of the bureaucracy.

This construction of the social service department with its unification of functions must be seen in line with the Bains Report, which was published in August 1972 and which reflected upon the necessary reforms in the overall management of local authorities. The central thrust of Bains was the introduction throughout local government of the practice of corporate management. This had been developed in the private sector of the USA and adopted by sections of British capital in the early 1960s. It represents an attempt to construct a centralised scientific management (Benington, 1976; Cockburn, 1977). The aim of the corporate approach is 'to look at the system as a whole, its goals, strategies and growth. It has regard to the pattern of relationships within an organisation to ensure efficient flows of information; to defining channels of responsibility and accountability, and to design processes so that different types of decision are taken at appropriate levels and in appropriate sequences' (Cockburn, 1977, p. 364).

Local government in one or two areas had introduced corporate management and had experienced a greatly heightened control over middle-level decision-making. This control and the form of control taken from capital itself was adopted by various committees appointed to examine all aspects of public accountability and government. The overall tendency throughout was to adopt *centralised* and *hierarchical* modes of management found in capitalist enterprises. Control and cheapness of service provision were taken from private enterprise and directly imposed upon local government structures.

In practical terms Bains envisaged the formation of a 'policy and resources committee' which would provide the general policy guidelines for the local authority. The parallel on the officers' side would be a management team of senior directors led by what has become known as the chief executive. This team usually meets *every* morning.

The introduction of the *structure* of corporate management went hand in glove with the introduction of a series of private enterprise management techniques, which have strengthened the centralised mode of control in local authorities. These techniques have come to be called by their initials, Mbo, O & M, etc. The total effect of these changes in the structure of the local state was to centralise control and policy formation to the *detriment of democracy*. Democracy was diminished in two distinct and important ways. This we emphasise since these changes structure the whole argument of our book. Democracy was lessened in terms of policy formation with councillors becoming less and less informed or in control of the day-to-day coustruction and implementation of 'their councils' policy. Secondly, the centralised control of management has limited the amount of day-to-day democracy that local authority *workers* can be involved in. It has directly reduced their autonomy. It is the renewed relationship between these two forms of democracy that we see socialists enlarging. John Benington notes that

> corporate management helps councillors to act as better managers of services and guardians of the public purse, but can undermine their role as representatives of political interests. Agenda of committees are increasingly being filled with material which has been identified, defined, analysed and presented for ratification almost entirely by technocrats. (1976, p. 114)

It is within this context that Seebohm needs to be understood. The overall merging of several departments obviously assisted this centralisation of local authority functions. Members of the Seebohm Committee were also aware, however, that the new department and its committee had to be large enough to construct an important place for itself in the local authority. 'Within local councils a committee responsible for the whole range of the personal social services would rank as a major committee' (para. 150). Thus one of the more dominant ideas in the Seebohm reconstruction was to try to combat other monolithic and powerful departments by creating a social service monolith that had the power to survive in the overall centralisation taking place.

There have been a number of consequences of this overall centralisation, most notably the fact that spending departments in local authorities are at the mercy of a much more efficient system of policy and financial *control*. The Association of Directors of Social Services has complained that in some authorities directors and social service committees

> are so subservient to other chief officers and committees that the concept of a statutory committee and a statutory officer as outlined by Seebohm is being thwarted. The effect of this is that a small group of directors of social services feel that they do not have effective control over vital aspects of the work of their department (*Social Work Today*, 8, 20, p. 2)

Many welfare workers may feel that it is a familiar obscuration for directors to claim that *they* do not have power. Yet here we are trying to explain that feeling, not only for directors, but for all those who work within social service departments. In Chapter 2 we outlined a massive programme of social and political change that was based upon an overall centralisation of power within the state. We are not claiming that the state was totally decentralised before, and that, say, children's officers could simply do what they liked. But we are saying that the feelings of increasing powerlessness experienced daily within social service departments are based upon a real structural centralisation which has shifted power not only away from the base within the department, but from the department to the policy advisory committee and from the local authority to central government.

We forget this overall process at our peril. It explains why there are some social service departments where, quite

genuinely, there is very little feeling of control anywhere in
the department over major service decisions. We are saying
that such a feeling reinforced by the structure of government, but we are also saying that this structure is only a part
of power both within social service departments and within
political power as a whole.

DECENTRALISATION, AREA TEAMS AND COMMUNITY

It may seem odd to have a heading about decentralisation
after a whole section stressing the massive centralisation of
power yet, as we have tried to stress, our analysis is based
upon a number of essential contradictions. The Seebohm
Report is a document riven with contradictions, and the
process of centralisation contained its opposite; for social
services cannot ever simply exist as a bureaucracy which
provides a form of controlled expenditure for monopoly
capital. It also has to provide a form of service which forces
it to come into direct contact with working-class people.

We have pointed out that working-class groups, including
the trade unions, were absent from the committee itself, but
we have also shown that all of the changes in state structure
that came about did so within a social democratic ideology
that forced the services to appreciate the need for some direct
contact with the lives of working people. Thus we talk about
the community dimension in the fields of planning, community development and education. In short, despite what many
welfare workers may occasionally feel, social service departments have to have some form of dynamic which brings them
into contact with working-class people.

As we will discuss later the Report had to come to terms
with the fact that millions of working people had *not* been
lifted out of poverty by the post-war welfare state; they still
experienced squalid and insecure conditions, and, within a
social democratic framework, these could not be simply
neglected. It was impossible to ignore the fact that social
services had to provide a much larger service to the mass of

the population and that this service would only take place if it was practically capable of delivering that service to working people.

One of the major and important innovations within this aspect of the Report was the construction of area teams to be placed as far as possible in the locality they were meant to serve. In the words of the Report, 'we attach great importance to a comprehensive area team approach in the search for an effective family social service and, as a concomitant, the delegation of the maximum authority to the area office' (HMSO, 1968, para. 592). These teams would become 'through training and experience, skilled at working with and in the community' (para. 507).

In practical terms, this section of the Report contradicts the stress on centralisation in the earlier section. It means that the Report was directly concerned in moving social work out into the community, in moving both its geographical site and its form closer to working-class people. As we shall see in Chapter 5 such a strategy affected many aspects of social policy in that period; in schools, in planning and in housing there was the direct introduction of the idea and practice of community work. This strategy reflected a whole range of problems, focusing mainly on the direct and obvious failure of the post-war welfare state to solve working people's problems, particularly in many of the inner-city areas.

As far as state workers are concerned this had direct and massive repercussions in the form and nature of social service provision. This decentralisation of services provided a relationship between service provider and client that had *three* basic progressive possibilities. First, locating teams away from the town hall in their own physical location and to some small extent with their own team autonomy provided a direct possible contradiction to the centralised bureaucratic power of not only the social service department but the corporate management structure of the whole local authority. Note that here we are talking of *possibilities* inherent in structures, not of inevitabilities. But the possibility of some low level organised autonomy was not an accidental outcome of Seebohm; rather it was an entirely intended consequence.

Secondly, decentralisation presented the possibility (again the *possibility*) of a closer relationship between social work area teams and the local community and its organisations. Indeed one whole chapter of Seebohm was written around this relationship. To quote: 'a clear responsibility then should be placed upon the social service department for developing conditions favourable to community identity and activity' (para. 483). In actuality of course such a relationship is far from being achieved but in all of our experiences within area teams that relationship is placed upon the team's agenda as a *worry*. Before Seebohm, such a possibility was not contained within the structures inherent in social service provision.

Thirdly, it represented the possibility of constructing work as a social service team. This provides us with a central focus in this chapter. We would put it forward as an essential principle of moving towards a socialist practice that welfare workers must work within a collective framework. Here though we must note that an inherent part of the Seebohm reorganisation put the *active possibility* of team work on the agenda of social workers.

To sum up, then, apart from the overall massive centralisation of local authority and social service departments that resulted from the Seebohm Report and within specific legislation passed after it, there was a contradiction in the structure that provided the possibility of a more progressive relationship both within the team of welfare workers and within the relationship between that team and the working-class people it works with.

STATE, FAMILY AND REPRODUCTION

Having looked at the politics behind the structure of Seebohm we would like to look also at the politics behind the provision of social service itself at the present political moment. This is crucial because Seebohm contains a new set of emphases which themselves represent a contradictory view of social service activity.

We would see this contradiction as between the enormous

emphasis on the role of the family in the family service of Seebohm, coupled with a recognition that most of the causes of the social problems that welfare workers came across were in themselves caused *not* by wrong ideas within the family but by structural problems within society. What does this latter statement mean?

In several sections of the Report and in statements made about the Report by its chairperson immediately afterwards, there was a particular emphasis upon the inequalities of our society that effected clients. Lord Seebohm himself emphasised this by saying that 60 per cent of all social service cases were caused by low income and bad housing (Sinfield, 1969). Similarly, in the Report itself, there is continual reference to the fact that there are severe inequalities which produce day-to-day insecurities for the working people that welfare workers meet. There is a hope that welfare workers and social service departments might intervene in these insecurities in such a way as to materially help people. But what do these statements mean?

In part it means that a state report recognised the basic structure of an unequal society and that that structure causes many people great hardship. We would suggest that in a capitalist society state documents will only *partially* recognise these facts and relationships. We would stress that documents such as Seebohm, the Plowden Report on primary education, the Children and Young Persons Act 1969 and the Beveridge Report during the war are forced by the collectivist politics of social democracy partially to recognise these structurally caused problems. This insight together with a lack of working-class power in a capitalist society stops short of ever putting forward structural changes to meet structurally caused problems. Here, what is important is to stress that *partial* recognition and to emphasise the fact that area social service teams rediscover this partial truth nearly every day of their practice but are *not* presented with a mode of structural intervention in those structural problems. Instead Seebohm enshrined (and practice since Seebohm has further enshrined) the role of an individualised family-centred service. Why is there this emphasis?

The family has been increasingly recognised by marxists over the past decade as one of the major instruments in the reproduction of capitalist social relationships. Althusser recognises the role of the family as one of the two major forms of ideological state apparatus (Althusser, 1970); feminist writing has stressed its role not just in the reproduction of female oppression but its central role in the reproduction of capitalism (Cockburn writes 'the state is dominant in the enterprise [of reproducing capitalist social relationships], but it cannot carry this out without the family' (1977, p. 59). Thus Seebohm's brief, 'to secure an effective family service', structures the whole aim of the service as a part of the family's reproductive role.

As we shall see in the next chapter the concrete relationship between social work practice and the family is far from one-dimensional itself. Sometimes the dominant ideology is to undermine various forms of the family, sometimes to bolster it. But the overall ideology and (again) *structure* of the service centres on the institution of the family, underlining its centrality to capitalist social relations.

We conclude this section however, by underlining the contradiction experienced daily by the welfare worker between an intervention purely within an individual family and a glimmer of recognition that nearly all the problems are caused by structures of inequality in our society.

DESKILLING, WELFARE WORK IN SOCIAL SERVICES, AND TRADE UNIONISM

Having outlined some of the contradictions that are contained within the very *structures* of the post-Seebohm social service departments, we would now like to comment on the way in which those structures have been *experienced within the practice of welfare work* itself. The main theme we will explore is the relationship between collective experience of practice and individualised experience.

For example we will explore the speed with which trade union activity and experience has affected these new departments and created a set of social relationships that are genuinely moving towards collectivism. As against this we will explore the increasing atomisation that has occurred within the work of social workers. We would stress that although these two trends are obviously in a very fierce tension with each other they are also, in a very real way, constructing each other. Thus increased individualisation and atomisation of the experience of work has acted as one of the major motive forces in the drive towards trade union activity and the movement away from a 'professional consciousness'. Similarly one of the ways in which the state bureaucracy has coped with that form of collectivisation has been to increase the atomised form of work and practice through organisation and methods techniques.

Let us start with the process that has come to be known as 'deskilling'. Braverman's book on *Labor and Monopoly Capital* (1974) is a part of a long tradition within marxism that comes to terms with the concrete way in which work is actually carried out. This is termed 'the labour process'; and although such a term may seem rather odd in direct relationship to welfare work, we would contend that this form of work does concretely contain labour and that the form that this labour takes is a process.

Braverman and others see one of the major forms of deskilling as being an increase in the distance between those who actually carry out the day-to-day aspects of the work and those who have an overall conception of that work. Thus, whilst many, many workers are involved in the process of building a small family car — some in digging the ore, some in smelting and finally some in driving the car to the dealer — the overall conception of what is happening in the construction of that car has become the property of a smaller and smaller number of people. One group, the workers, has grown in number for each product, and another group, those with an overview of producing a car, has got smaller.

We would see this process as having a direct, central and biting relevance to welfare work. The Seebohm departments, as we have said, have increased their heirarchy and their authoritarian nature. We have suggested that this *form* has been directly lifted from the private enterprise arena where its main aim has been to increase control by a central management team. As well as control, the function of this management is to co-ordinate, and it will become immediately recognisable within social service departments that this controlling and co-ordinating function is carried out by the same small band of high echelon managers. Indeed, in welfare work the controlling function is carried out *through* the co-ordinating function. This is in part because welfare work in all its ramifications is, in fact, very difficult to control. It is difficult to control what a worker says to a client in their own home. Direct practical control will sometimes take place, like the checking of all letters before they are sent out, but more usually control is exercised through the 'planning' and 'co-ordination' of concrete resources and where they will be deployed. Such planning is carried out by a hierarchy that excludes rank-and-file welfare workers.

The exclusion of welfare workers from this role reproduces another feature of private enterprise, the division between mental and manual labour. Such an emphasis may seem odd when initially applied to social work since we think of all welfare workers as non-manual workers. Here, though, the split is about knowledge of the whole process involved in the work. Some people have to carry out the work of the organisation and others plan it: *the two groups are inevitably split* and do not have a cross membership. Thus above team leaders there are very few people who ever *meet clients*; below team leaders there are very few people who are structurally allowed to plan or co-ordinate. This does not imply that welfare work becomes purely manual, in the same way that dock work or mining or domestic labour actually includes *mental* labour. But we would underline the increasingly dominant trend in welfare work that separates control and practice further and further.

Thirdly, we would emphasise the way in which social work departments have encouraged the adoption of increasingly sophisticated management techniques that have reduced the day-to-day power of rank-and-file welfare workers. Kogan and Terry (1971) emphasise the need 'to pay heed to efficiency, out-put, budgeting, economy, clarity of organisation and other managerial virtues' (1971, p. 6). Similarly directors of the new departments are continually expected to 'be familiar with modern management techniques'. What does this mean for workers with clients?

There is no doubt that this increasing sophistication has assumed a greater and greater control over the day-to-day 'caring process'.

> A department cannot be certain that it is functioning effectively unless there is a significant correspondence between filed activity on the one hand and overall departmental policy, as decided during priority setting, objectives setting, and budget making on the other. (Gould, 1976, p. 1182; see also Braverman, 1974, Chapter 4)

This has meant a direct correspondence within departments with a form of information gathering for the management and the way in which day-to-day practice is noted and controlled. A department's work can now be summed up in a page of computer print-out within a variety of management constructed categories which dominate the thinking and practice of the department.

The features we have discussed so far have been internal to social workers, control over their work. We have so far stressed the increasing power of management in this process and before we turn to the countervailing tendency of increased trade union activity we would underline other trends that have affected welfare workers but which are external to the welfare process. For example the depression of wages in the welfare sector in relationship to other areas of labour have had an effect upon workers' consciousness. Poulantzas has maintained that factors such as these have had a particular effect on the class determination of 'the subaltern agents in the public and private bureaucratised sector'. This process has been noted by industrial sociologists as a 'proletarianisation' of white-collar workers. We will now turn to the actual experience of this amongst social workers.

But first let us summarise what we have said so far about the new social service departments.

First, we have outlined the increased centralisation of the departments and have gone on to discuss the way in which welfare workers are increasingly forced into a more powerless position within the departments: a position which leaves them carrying out policy in a detailed way whilst having no real control over that policy; a position which increasingly atomises and individualises their work both in relationship to each other and their clients. We then discussed the necessary contradiction within the *structure* of the Seebohm departments which underlines the need for a decentralised area teams. This structure provides the possibility of progressive practice within the departments concerned; progressive in so far as it has a closer relationship with the day-to-day organisation of working people in localities; progressive in so far as it has the possibility of providing a counterweight in these area teams to balance the increased bureaucracy; progressive in so far as it provides the possibility of a collective team practice and experience. We see all three of these progressive *possibilities* as directly cutting across the powerful deskilling process that we then outlined. We will now turn to *how* we see that happening.

TRADE UNION ACTIVITY, COLLECTIVE ACTION AND WELFARE WORKERS

We turn now to changes in a very different set of institutions, that is within the collective working-class organisation of trade unions. Such a story is usually separated from the changes in the state structures and experience of social work but it is essential to both the analysis and the prescriptions of this book that they are dealt with in close relationship to each other. This is because we see the trade union movement as an integral part of the struggle for a socialist welfare practice. Consequently we will spend some time on the actual experience of trade union activity for welfare workers as well as the historical, global importance of such institutions. To carry out this analysis we will start with an analysis of the social workers' strikes of 1978—9.

The social work strike 1978—9

In mid-1978 state-employed social workers became involved

in the first social work strike to affect more than one authority. This strike showed social workers in a number of authorities turning to a traditional working-class mode of struggle
for the first time; this involved pickets, union ballots, working
within a federal union to maximise support; strike pay and
negotiations. But above all it involved a day-by-day collective
experience for hundreds of welfare workers; an experience
which we believe runs directly against many individualised
practice experiences.

The analysis here tries to explore the contradiction between
these different experiences; on the one hand an individualised,
deskilled hierarchical experience; on the other a collective
experience with aspects of direct democracy and the learning
of new and varied skills. In so doing we would *not* want to
say that everyone who went on strike from social services
went through an experience which totally transformed them;
which revolutionised the whole way in which they approach
their job; which transformed their politics. Rather we want
to portray a different theory of learning, one that sees such
contradictory experiences as providing an important part of
life, which can be built upon. We will conclude the chapter by
discussing the way in which trade unionism and a collective
approach to social work can build on this and can be a basis
for socialist welfare work.

The background to the strike

In 1976 the NALGO conference passed a motion giving local
authority social workers the right to negotiate locally with
their employers. The demand was resisted by the employers
despite the fact that in a variety of other areas NALGO had
won the right for their members to negotiate locally.

Such situations reflect the strengths and the weaknesses of
a union such as NALGO. As a federal union representing
many different sorts of public service workers it forces welfare
workers to become involved at least with other local authority
workers. Such an imperative ensures that any form of trade
union action by social workers must immediately take them
outside of their professional circle of colleagues and allies. It
must bring them into contact, as equals in terms of union

membership, with clerks and middle-level management in a whole range of local authority services; it forces them to make a case about welfare work to these people. We must not underestimate the importance of this to our theoretical and political approach, since welfare workers have no choice but to popularise and deprofessionalise issues in NALGO, and for many welfare workers this is their first ever experience of linking welfare work with other people and other organisations.

However, it also reveals certain weaknesses that are contained within the dialectic of this federal union. When an issue arises, such as this strike, a federal union almost automatically reveals itself as a very split structure. In the end the union spent over £3 million on strike pay for social workers; an expenditure and a commitment on this scale made it very difficult for, say, clerks in the housing department or middle management in the treasurer's department to see it as a correct use of union funds and strength to back up one small part of the membership. Consequently there was a constant possibility during the strike that a larger section of the union would believe that their interests were being sold short by supporting the social workers. Both locally and nationally a federal union on strike demands very strong trade union consciousness from its members. This is especially true over a long period – and this strike continued for three months in some areas.

In August 1978, the social workers in Newcastle struck because the management in that authority refused to negotiate locally. Over the next five months, fifteen other local authorities joined them in this dispute. The strike was a long and bitter one, lasting until March 1979 when the emergency committee of the union starting sending social workers back to work often against the wishes of that particular group of workers. The particular issues and the outcome of the dispute, the formal terms, do not really concern us here. Importantly, though, the issue of local bargaining as against national bargaining is one that does have a relevance to our analysis. From the middle of the 1960s national private enterprise organisations started to try to move towards industry bargaining as against local bargaining. This represented another form of centralisation, in that it took the arena of struggle further away from the local shopfloor, from the plant, and placed it in a national setting. Of course the various income policies took it out of the national industry setting and placed it in the setting of state-run policy thereby attempting to withdraw the outcome from all kinds of struggle.

What is important here however is that NALGO were prepared to move against that trend, which must have represented some form of faith in the power of local union strength to carry out local negotiations and to drive them to a successful local outcome. Indeed the struggle itself showed the great strength of local associations in backing strike action and the amazing solidarity of the social workers themselves.

SOCIAL WORK AND TRADE UNION CONSCIOUSNESS

Although social workers had generally been members of NALGO for many years they had had little impact upon the union either in policy or action. Given this, there was no immediate or obvious evidence that social workers favoured a federal trade union. Indeed, just before the strike started the British Association of Social Workers (BASW) had decided that the affiliation of social workers to NALGO was so tenuous that it was now a good time to start a union of their own (BUSW).

Therefore it is necessary to answer the question about the support for the strike amongst social workers by looking theoretically at the relationship. In the section above we outlined the way in which a centralised form and structure of welfare work had constructed a deskilled and individualised workforce. This experience, we suggested, stripped away the veils of ideology around such things as 'professional autonomy'. It increased the welfare workers' perception of themselves as workers. It is a difficult and very tight dialectic that we are trying to explain here. First, we are stressing the objective process of proletarianisation which turns people into pure members of the labour force and we are suggesting that this process has increased in magnitude over the recent period. Secondly, subjectively we are suggesting that this set

of experiences has a direct impact upon workers' consciousness in that it works against some of the practice relationships
that they develop with their colleagues. In work that did
have an overall professional ideology binding it together a
tension emerged between the new forms of work experience
and this professional ideology; people do not 'feel' that they
are a professional collective in relationship to each other
because of their qualifications, or as individual autonomous
workers as against the normal management. This experience
then begins to mirror increasingly the normal experience of
labour in a capitalist society. That experience on a day-to-day
basis constructs a different form of collectivity around the
trade union movement; around forms of experience and
struggle which overcome that atomised experience. It is this
collectivity that is the bedrock experience of trade unionism,
and which social workers began to express in the lead up to
the strike of 1978—9.

We want to underline this experience here since trade
unionism is usually characterised for welfare workers as a
very mechanical activity. It is about large anonymous meetings; about smoke-filled rooms; about male dominated
aggressive confrontation, and so on. It is undoubtedly true
that trade unionism does contain these experiences but they
are not the *essence* of the activity. What constructs trade
union consciousness and activity is the move towards collective experience and collective activity in a work environment
that is essentially individualising and with an employer and a
management and a society that wants continually to maintain
that individual experience as the *only* way of coming to work.

So precisely what did the strike do in relationship to this?
First, we do not want to repeat simplistic generalisations
about every social worker's life: we are talking about readily
recognisable trends in activity and experience. In the locality
where the strikes actually occurred the social workers, in
order to gain the support of the rest of their branch of
NALGO, had to act collectively in one way or another. This
was done on the backs of an ever growing shop stewards'
organisation, which needs some explaining. From the early
1970s social workers began to develop a form of union
organisation around what we initially called representatives.
In a number of places these consisted of a representative

elected by a team or a home which then went to a representatives' meeting to discuss the issues in the whole department.
These issues could then be taken to the NALGO branch.
Such an organisation may seem obvious and simple yet it
represents one of the unique features of British trade unionism. It allows each area of a workforce to have its own elected
voice and it allows those voices to meet and talk to construct
a policy. We would suggest that such a structure provides a
vitally important counterweight to the structure imposed by
management. It is not a simple thing; it needs constant
reaffirmation, but it does provide the material bedrock of a
very different collective experience of a social service department.

Apart from the shop stewards' organisation a great deal of
decision-making took place in mass meetings, either mass
meetings of the social workers or branch meetings. The former
represented a real democratic forum where a decision could
be made and then carried out. In this setting many probably
had their first major experience of direct democracy carried
out in a collective way. The second, the branch meeting,
represented a much wider meeting where social workers were
forced to make out their case to their fellow trade unionists.
Here a wider form of collectivity was experienced.

The activity of striking was not a simple passive withdrawal
of labour. One of the continuing important activities that it
involved was picketing. Picketing has always been a vitally
important part of working-class strike activity. It involves
different sorts of confrontation at different times. For example
the miners never really have to picket their own members or
stop materials going into and out of the pits, but they have very
successfully used the weapon of picketing to stop the movement of coal. Picketing then takes these different forms and
contains different appeals; you need to appeal initially to the
solidarity of the workers in your own place of work; secondly
to fellow trade unionists who move goods and services in and
out of your place of work. Here you are asking them to put
trade union solidarity over and above the orders from their
own management to deliver this or that good.

For the NALGO social workers' strike, the experience of
picketing was vital *both* in terms of the effectiveness of the
dispute and in terms of the overall experience of trade union

collectivity. There is no feeling quite like standing in the snow on the steps of a town hall with three other social workers and turning away a tanker full of fuel for the boilers at six in the morning. Picketing contains a whole range of important lessons and experiences concerned with solidarity and collective activity. It contains experiences that are unique within a social worker's experience. Such feelings do not easily go away; more particularly, they do not have to be personally experienced by the individual to feel that emotional impact. It was *our* picket line and not mine or me that stopped it.

The essence of the whole participatory strike experience is that it is forced to be anti-individualistic in its impact and form. There is a lot of discussion and experience which goes beyond the individualism of the office. In direct contrast to the atomised, privatised work experience, you want and need to share a great deal about your 'work' on strike.

What is the direct effect of this?

At least it constructs a contradiction between usual work and strike experience but here we are discussing building upon that contradiction rather than simply noting it. To make this point we want to look closely at one particular locality to make sense of the movements and changes there and then try to generalise from that.

We want to stress that there is no automatic movement from an experience of trade unionism to a more overt political understanding of welfare work. For many the experience of trade union action is kept in a different experiential category from their work experience. What we have stressed is that the increasing individualisation of work actually plays a role in *constructing* the collective trade union response; we cannot guarantee that everyone will *experience* it that way.

THE LEEDS ACTION: FROM DEFENCE TO OFFENSIVE COLLECTIVITY

In Leeds the 1978—9 strike lasted sixteen weeks and involved about 90 per cent of all area office field workers. 'Involved', in this case, means at the level of activity and experience around picketing and meetings and constant discussion. As in most white-collar strikes of the late 1970s there were people who became totally transformed by the experience from self-effacing quiet workers to chairpersons of strike committees. These were individual stories; what is important to us here is the fact that there was a collective movement by many of the welfare workers that could *only* have taken place because of the collective strike experience.

During the action there was much discussion not just of the issue at stake but about the nature of social services in Leeds. This discussion took a number of forms; most of it was a longer version of the day-to-day moaning that goes on in all welfare offices and must provide the mainspring for any collective alternative action (Corrigan, 1980). But because people were on *strike* it went beyond this. On strike the welfare workers were actually experiencing some form of collective strength. They took part in activities that challenged the right of social work management to manage. They challenged the view of the world that management put forward, they did it through press releases, though a newspaper, through meetings and through pickets.

Here they were not simply moaning about their jobs but were doing things about it in a sophisticated way; in a way that claimed they had the *right* to talk about social work. As much right as management in the town hall. Contained *within* this activity was the beginnings of an alternative view not only of conditions of service but of social service itself. For the challenge to management's rights to manage on a day-to-day basis does contain the possibility of a challenge to their right to define what social service actually is.

We would contend that such a challenge is different from the nature of the challenge put forward by a professional consciousness. It is true and important that the British Association of Social Workers does put forward alternative views of practice to that of management. What is important here is the way in which the alternatives that were generated by the strike come out of a different set of social relationships and therefore have a different set of possibilities contained within them. Why is this the case? In the middle of trade union action, the nature of the social relationships between welfare worker and welfare worker; between welfare worker and fellow trade unionist; between welfare worker and welfare management change radically. They contain elements of solidarity between some people and opposition to others; this solidarity cuts across from those working purely within welfare to other workers; the opposition is opposition to those who always claim they too have the best interests of the client at heart, the management. Views of welfare constructed within this framework are much more likely to look for some of the meaning and their strength to other workers and *not* to the experts in the department or the profession.

This has an obvious importance to our argument in this book. We oppose the way in which social democracy hands all the intellectual and practical power over welfare to the 'expert'. Here we can see a process which challenges this not only within welfare work but by possibly involving other trade unionists and clients as well. This goes beyond the social democratic form of policy construction to the germ of a socialist form of welfare policy.

In Leeds, as the strike progressed, a number of social workers started to see the wider need to formulate detailed plans for welfare in the city. Here we must make the point that apart from the management of social services — the experts — Leeds like every other city had no other detailed plans for social services. It was true that the political parties had one or two lines in their local manifesto, but no one had constructed a policy. The Leeds Social Workers Action Group decided to break the monopoly that management enjoyed and construct a pamphlet on the levels of service in Leeds.

The contents of the pamphlet are not material to us here; the way it was constructed and its aftermath are. There are several ways in which knowledge of social services exist in a city. Obviously in terms of official local authority statistics; also other forms of statistical knowledge; welfare workers themselves have a knowledge of social services; clients have a knowledge and so to do the general public. Nearly all of it is knowledge that is totally unorganised: the role of alternative plans is to construct this knowledge around a political dimension.

Crucially the Social Workers Action Group (SWAG) grew out of the strike and out of the trade union movement. Consequently it looked to a number of different dimensions for its strength and its information. The first pamphlet was signed by a number of social workers and they came under some threat about the utilisation of material gained from their job. Consequently the rest were published by the NALGO branch secretary; this change was an important one, since it put the social workers' plans at the core of the trade union movement. Organically SWAG had grown out of that movement and it made sure that one of its major political targets was that movement; in the end it is hoped that variations on such pamphlets become the property and the policy of the working-class movement.

What does this mean? First, it means that welfare trade unionists and workers can construct an alternative policy to that of management. Such a process is important; such a result (the policy) is also important. The process matters because it shows welfare workers that collectively they do have a knowledge of the *whole* department. This is important because, as we note on p. 65, the process of deskilling has taken away from the actual worker any overall knowledge of the social service. Each individual carries out only a section of that work and management can always claim that the individual worker does not have the whole picture. Collectively welfare workers have a sharper, more realistic knowledge of the department than management can ever construct. They have a living, moving, day-to-day picture; unfortunately it exists purely at the level of individualised experience *unless it is brought together*. Thus such activities can *only* be constructed by the collective appreciation of all workers in the department.

Secondly the process involves not just all workers as fellow welfare workers, but also as workers and trade unionists. This means that if such organisations are taken seriously (and we have suggested that the industrial action *forced* the social workers to take them seriously through the action of picketing), then the source and direction of the overall view of welfare policy is other working-class organisations. Such a process is not easy, but it means that when you turn away from a trade union meeting because you see it as 'irrelevant' or reject a meeting about play in the community on the grounds that it is 'not your concern' there is *no* alternative but to go back to such organisations again and again.

But it is not only the collective process of the policy construction that is important. It is also vital to see the resulting policies as a real change in welfare politics. For once one group has constructed some policies in relationship with working people, then the myth that there is only one objective policy for social service — that propounded by the experts in the Town Hall — is dead. It means that others can pick up the possibility of struggling around these alternatives; it means that the managements cannot simply claim that they are the only ones with the overview. They now have to contend with a well informed overall policy that is backed up and believed in by a number of working-class organisations who, it is to be hoped, increasingly will have constructed part of the policy. It is within such relationships that the beginnings of socialist welfare work are to be found.

COLLECTIVITY AND TEAMS

This chapter has been built around the contradiction in the relationships of the Seebohm departments. Part of that contradiction is between an increasingly individualised experience of work and the resulting collectivity of trade unions.

Collective political organisations such as SWAG can provide an overall opportunity for discussion of practice at a collective level, but there has to be a day-to-day organisation which can overcome the basic experience of individualisation. Earlier in the chapter we outlined the way in which it was essential for Seebohm (within its social democratic framework) to construct area teams. Similarly in residential work there has been an increase in the role of staff meetings.

Therefore, *within* the structure of social services there is a form of collective work envisaged by social service departments and we have tried to show this as an essential part of the structure as envisaged by management and Seebohm. Any readers who have spent any time in welfare work will recognise that the actual experience of 'team work' is in nearly every case an extremely patchy and attenuated experience. There are very few welfare workers who look to their teams as a major source of collective support in their day-to-day practice. By and large the individualisation of practice within the Seebohm departments represents the major experience; it is left to workers on their own to contend with such difficulties as the work throws up. Of course friendships amongst fellow team workers help a lot, but it is very rare for the team as a team to provide this function.

However, there are no ways forward for progressive practice without the creation of a real team approach to welfare work. This is true since, either area teams or staff as a whole in a residential home can only relate to their area or their home through their collective understanding and appreciation of the totality. There is no way in which an *individual* can embrace a community or collective approach to the area; that can only be realistically achieved by a whole team approaching its collective task. Otherwise the members of the team as individuals are doomed to a very individualised appreciation of the problems of the area or home. This has a number of vitally important implications for progressive practice. As long as a team experiences its area as individuals; as long as a staff experience the population of a resident establishment purely as individuals, then the possibilities for any progressive practice in the area or home will be *severely* limited.

We are talking then of an essential prerequisite for progressive practice. Why is this so? The most important reason is to be found in the inevitable power relationship between worker and client. As long as that relationship remains at an individual level it will not be possible for the client to operate with anything but the most violent reactive power against the worker. Individual clients quite rightly find it enormously difficult to provide a coherent co-operative criticism of practice. Such a criticism can only be achieved through collective organisation or collective locality culture. In these circumstances it may be possible for groups of clients within a locality to construct a very different understanding and relationship to the team.

Secondly team work is vital because it provides the possibility of detailed day-to-day support. Such support cannot be provided by a city-wide group of welfare workers; nor can it be provided by the trade union branch. It has to exist at the level of day-to-day practice.

Consequently we feel that the struggle for team work is essential. Unfortunately team work within welfare work is usually treated in a dual way, either as something that is easy or something that is impossible. We would say that team work is extremely difficult but possible and vital. One of the first prerequisites for its construction is to understand this difficulty and to appreciate all the problems that obstruct successful team work. Some of our earlier discussion on Seebohm and deskilling is important here, since it shows the power behind individualisation.

There is, however, also an ideological component to the problem. From both the left and the right there is real difficulty in constructing a proper relationship of comradeship with colleagues. From the right comes the image of professionalism, closely identified with a person's capacity to make 'correct' decisions. The image of professionalism is compounded by the training process that most welfare workers go through which also individualises the worker's task. From the left there is a distrust of colleagues who do not hold a left position – a series of labels. This means progressives can come across as arrogant, dismissive know-alls.

How can we overcome these difficulties? We would suggest that there are two solid sets of experiences which allow the workers to plan for the construction of a more collective team work. First – a point we have already made – the rise of trade unionism provides some form of common collective experience. Not, as we have said many times, that this automatically provides the base for collective team work, but where it has occurred it does provide a *form* of collective experience which greatly assists the possibility of team work. Secondly, it is widely recognised and agreed that it is only be collectivising the appreciation of the practice involved in an area that there will be any real understanding of 'the community'. Neither of these two material experiences ensures that team work is constructed, but they do provide some form of counterweight to the power of the individuation process.

CONCLUSIONS

We have tried to make specific the overall analysis of the restructured social democratic state. We have tried to show that Seebohm was riven with important contradictions; these were imposed by the overall social democratic framework.

However the contradictions cannot be resolved in a progressive way if they are dealt with within a social democratic political and practice process. We suggest that there are material experiences with trade unionism and in collective work that provide for the possibility of a socialist process of policy and practice discussion and implementation. This will only be fully achieved by the full involvement of working-class organisations in the whole political process of personal social services.

4
Child Care Decisions – Intervention and the Law

INTRODUCTION

In looking at welfare *work* we have tried to extend the usual simplistic emphasis on client/worker interaction styled 'practice'. So in the previous chapter we would contend that we were talking about practice, even if that practice seems to be primarily concerned with organisation and fellow workers. Our analysis and our discussions of the work try to overcome the simplistic categorisation and dichotomy of the experience of 'being a worker', distinguished from the experience of 'delivering a service'. Nowhere is this more crucial than in this chapter on child care. It would be easy to slip here into an analysis and a description purely of client/worker interaction, with a discussion of policy and organisation 'dealt with elsewhere'. In fact of course writing in such a way would only have presented an 'idealised' view of practice; one that takes place entirely out of a context. Yet to describe the context in too simple a way sees 'context' as something that totally structures the possibilities of practice and is therefore deterministic.

We wish to approach this chapter by looking at some different influences on child care decisions, trying to underline that all these influences contain crucial contradictions. The contradictions in policy do not simply exist at that level; neither do contradictions in ideology simply work themselves through in people's heads; similarly practice takes place in detailed structures, such as case conferences, which are massively effected by both sets of contradictions. In line with our analysis above, we do not simply want to see these contradictions as the result of a series of humane intentions but as coming from the way in which various differing pressures have impinged on the development of child care policy at different times.

Therefore we start this chapter with a discussion of the development of child care policy in the 1960s. Specifically we focus on the legal aspects of the policy to try to bring out some of the contradictions that exist even in the state form of a 'law'. Secondly, we look at the ideology of childhood that dominates not just welfare workers but most of our society. This is important since there are many unquestioned assumptions about children and the way in which we treat them. These are simply taken from the settings of 'common sense' and grafted on to both law and practice. We will question these assumptions not by posing a different ideology but by pointing to the significantly differing aspects within the existing one.

Thirdly, we will look at the way in which the structures of practice have been formed within welfare; such structures as case conferences, supervision sessions and aspects of structured autonomy which do exist within the child/welfare worker relationship. From this we will discuss different aspects of existing practice. Fairly obviously springing as they do from different aspects of contradictions, these practices are themselves fractured and pragmatic. They are usually experienced in the welter of guilt caused by the combination of feeling that one really should be able to help the child but cannot; and a cynical dismissal of the job because the structures do not seem to allow any form of real welfare response. Having tried to show how these contradictions arise from state structures we then go on to discuss alternatives and how those contradictions provide the possibility of moving towards a socialist child care.

THE POLICY CONTEXT

The 1969 Children and Young Persons Act is one part of a body of law on children which fits together as a whole. This body of law has been built up and developed over the past 100 years or more. Its development has two aspects. The first is the progressive modification of the criminal law in its application to children. The second is the development of provisions for the care of children, culminating in the establishment in 1948 of the children's departments of local authorities and the conferment on those authorities in 1963 of an express duty to undertake preventative work with children and their families. The 1969 Act carries these developments, and the integration of legal and social provisions for the care and control of children one stage further. (HMSO, 1969)

Many social policy studies have identified the growth of the welfare state over the last 150 years as part of mankind's inevitable, humane and progressive movement towards a better society. It will be evident by now that we would not accept this analysis. In this section we want to illustrate the nature of the social forces which have constructed child care policy in this country. This approach challenges the view that child care policy has been inevitably 'progressive' by placing the development of that policy in the context of the economic, political and ideological struggles which took place around it. This analysis is vital as it helps us to understand the arena in which child care practice takes place. We hope to show that this arena contains crucial contradictions which make possible the struggle for alternative forms of practice.

The first piece of legislation relating to children who were orphaned, neglected or vagrant was the 1601 Poor Law. Until 1948 children 'deprived of a normal home life' were cared for either in the work houses, in homes and approved schools, by boarding out, or by the various voluntary bodies. For the working class in nineteenth-century Britain the crucial experience of state 'welfare' policy was that of the Poor Law. There is, indeed, strong evidence that the principles enshrined in 1834 are still alive and well in many aspects of social policy today (Ginsburg, 1979). However these practices have come under increasing attack from the working class and the liberal welfare lobby. The basic theme in child care policy in the last century has been a retreat from the principles of the Poor Law.

THE 1948 CHILDRENS ACT

In 1946 the Curtis Committee reported on 'existing methods of providing for children who from loss of parents or from any cause whatever are deprived of a normal home life with their own parents or relatives'. The Committee advocated that new provision was needed to 'compensate the child for the effects of deprivation by providing him with the right kind of physical and emotional environment in which he could develop his natural potential'.

This principle was embedded in the 1948 Childrens Act. The Act represented a break with the Poor Law as the newly formed children's departments were to assess the need of the child rather than to adminster a test of destitution. This 'break' is crucial to an understanding of child care legislation.

Before and throughout the nineteenth century social policy had a crucial role to play in the 'moral regulation' of the poor (see, for example, Corrigan and Corrigan, 1978; Corrigan, 1981). This policy had two orientations. First, some elements of policy were designed to transform the whole life-style of the lower classes — say, for example, public health or educational legislation. Secondly, other elements were concerned with particular sub-groupings of deviants or 'dangerous' sections.

By and large most of the policies dealt with the working class as a whole through mass schooling, sanitation and the Poor Law, rather than selecting specific class groupings. However, each of these policies was also concerned with the increasing internal differentiation of the lower classes within this *overall* policy. Thus the Poor Law, whilst it was aimed at the construction of the whole labour force in an overarching manner, was also concerned with the *specific* punishment of unemployment or any form of labour indiscipline. Similarly the education system was constructed to deal with the whole class but began to develop its own legal methods for punishing and stigmatising groups who 'failed' to assimilate the full gamut of bourgeois values.

What is important about the social policy of this period is that it functioned quite clearly as a policy of social intervention — it had as its object distinct social groups rather than individual human subjects. State social policy in the nineteenth century did not attempt to change the individual attitudes of people through individualised interventions. Nor was the state interested in the incremental improvement which comes from 'inter-personal' intervention by individual state agents.

The 1948 Childrens Act differentiates itself from this nineteenth-century social policy by looking at the individualised needs of each child and by constructing a specialised and individualised service based on social casework to meet these needs. A major influence in this field was the ideology which informed the child care officers themselves. This ideology sees the cause of delinquency and abnormal personality as being largely a function of inadequate mothering in the early years of life. (It is noteworthy that the list of evidence given to the Curtis Committee includes that of a Lt Col John Bowlby!) This form of practice and ideology found easy acceptance in the period of the post-war boom. After all, poverty was no longer a major problem. It followed that acts of deviance were explained predominantly as individual and pathological problems. Thus instead of seeking change through broad-ranging social policies, the focus changed to adjusting malfunctioning individuals and their families. Delinquency was seen by the social democratic policy-makers as stemming from 'psychological maladjustment'; in an age of consensus it was not possible to relate such manifestations to more fundamental social problems.

Of course it would be falling straight into the consensus trap to neglect the presence of the working class in the construction of social policies — including the child care field.

The Labour government that was elected following the Second World War was brought to power by a significant radicalisation of the working class following the war. However the government also reflected all the contradictions of social democracy: a reliance on the working class to bring it to power, but a fundamental mistrust of building any directly democratic base within the class; a commitment to social change, but always within the context of capitalism; a dependence on the state to bring about this change, but without an analysis of the limitations on the state.

The 1948 Act embodied the firm comitment by the Labour Party to compensating children for the deprivations that they suffered and underlining the importance of the correct family unit as the model for child rearing. The Act was constructed with a minimal understanding of why the need arose for such policy; it had no political view of where such deprivation came from; of the political and economic context in which child-rearing took place in a capitalist society. The Act was primarily created by the experience of the Second World War. The war had two direct effects upon the image of child-rearing in the UK. First, through evacuation, the full extent of material deprivation and its brutalising effect became clear to a wider public audience. Secondly, it constructed a situation, like most total wars, where the future was seen to belong to children. Mothers and babies became a central part of the war effort. Equally, the aftermath of the war saw an increase in the numbers of children born into single-parent families. A large standing army, let alone the invasion of GIs, ensured that a significant group of children were born outside of the two-parent nuclear family. These factors highlighted for a social democratic government the need for child care policy even if there was no true understanding of what was causing this deprivation.

THE CHILDREN AND YOUNG PERSONS ACT 1963

The 1963 Children and Young Persons Act was very ambitious in its aims. The policy-makers hoped to get children's departments to combat juvenile delinquency and promote the welfare of children by helping the family as a whole to function 'properly'. The main change in the provisions of this Act was that local authorities would be given statutory obligations to provide advice, guidance and material assistance to promote the welfare of the child thereby diminishing the need for reception into care. The necessity of *preventive* work with families, as opposed to merely the 'rescue' work that was possible under the constraints of the 1948 Act was beginning to gain some credence. Why was it necessary to construct a new Act? The main factor was the combination of real increases in juvenile delinquent behaviour and the amplification of this reality through moral panic. The late 1950s and the early 1960s saw the growth of concern for youth that had been constructed not just by the war itself but by the social conditions of the post-war world. Such a background stimulated greater interest since delinquency or deprivation as a result of war could be easily understood in simple structural terms. The was caused dislocation and dislocation had harmful effects on children's lives. However, the fact that it seemed to get worse at a time when it was believed that 'poverty' had been done away with; that there was equality of opportunity and an 'affluent society', caused a much bigger analytical and political problem. It was the continuation and increase in this problem that forced the restructuring of child care policy over this period.

THE CHILDREN AND YOUNG PERSONS ACT 1969

In this section we hope to illustrate the political context in which the 1969 Act came about.

John Clarke (1979) has argued that a 'social coalition existed around child care and practice' that was instrumental in bringing the 1969 Act on to the statute book. This coalition consisted of key figures in the parliamentary Labour Party, organised professional interest groups and groups of Fabian academics. Together these three wings of the social coalition constructed a welfarist position which could claim some social scientific rigour and respectability, a genuine engagement with child care practice and effective leverage for political power. This alliance proved so effective as to gain a dominant position throughout the latter half of the 1960s.

This coalition coincided with the development of certain powerful trends in social democratic thought. In 1964 the Longford Report had proposed the abolition of the juvenile court: 'No child in early adolescence should have to go through criminal proceedings; these children should receive the treatment they need without any stigma' (Longford, 1964). The Report did not tackle the political and economic issues which lay at the basis of many of the dilemmas that it confronted. The key problems identified in the Report, which formed the basis of the 1965 White Paper *The Child the Family and the Young Offender*, were a 'weakening of moral fibre, and legal and social stigma against working class youths' and crime committed by the 'inadequate and immature', who require a restoration of their 'self-respect' and 'a training in respect for the rights of others' (Longford, 1964, pp. 4–6). Here then, in the specific context of developing social policies relevant to juvenile and adult crime is a clear expression of the Labour Party's more general commitment to the 'common good'. For though the working-class youths are to derive some benefit from such policies, their ultimate justification is the eradication of the forms of deviancy which threaten social harmony. These themes dominated Labour politicians' attitudes up to the passing of the Act.

Opposition to the 1965 White Paper was strong — it came from 'vested interest groups' such as the magistrates, the police, probation officers and the Tory Party. The 'failure' of the 1965 White Paper was, however, very far from complete. Many of its radical suggestions — such as the substantial extension of the use of care, protection and control procedures for children up to seventeen years — survived into the 1968–9 debates. Why then did the 1969 Act get onto the statute books when only four years earlier reform had been stopped?

We would suggest that the balance of crucial political forces had changed in the intervening years. In 1965 the supporters of the White Paper were fragmented and low key in their campaign. Without the open and to some degree co-ordinated backing of some committed interest groups, a social democratic government found it difficult to resist the combined hostility of so many prestigious and well-established groups. By the time *Children in Trouble* appeared the professional wing of the welfarist coalition had learnt important lessons. These included increasing their own internal coherence, tightening links between on the one hand the academic and practice wings of the coalition and on the other the Labour Party in government. It also tailored its proposals around the strengths and weaknesses of the opposition.

Backing given by key academics and especially professional interest groups provided an essential complement to the direct committed political activity of the Labour government. This time they held firm. Thus the 1969 Children and Young Persons Act was forced onto the statute book by a Labour government whose respect for 'expertise' capable of 'serving the nation as a whole' had led it to a dependency on Fabian academics and social work professionals. This alliance and the perspectives contained within it may have been 'progressive' but were in both ideology and practice a long way from the needs and aspirations of the working-class children and parents. Deeply built into the conventional 'welfarist' thinking of the time was a negative but highly influential assumption that organised representations of working-class opinion had no place in the debate on juvenile delinquency or in the machinery determining responses to it.

It is possible that if working-class organisations had been involved in the framing of the Act then it would have been less 'liberal' in intent; but it is also likely that the simple welfarist and family notions of causation would have met with some other structural forms of explanation. What is significant is that in confronting such powerful opposing forces the Labour Party did not develop a broadly-based and explicitly political alliance. Instead it relied upon experts who had 'specialist skills'. This is all the more politically blinkered since it was at this time that other academics in criminology were trying to get beyond the family pathology model to look at the interests of clients and the working class as a whole (Cohen, 1971).

The resulting legislation therefore had to rely heavily upon the limited perceptions of both intervention and causation that such an academic coalition could muster. There was little analysis of real power in the theories and practice that arose from this coalition, and consequently there was no clear understanding of the power being handed out to welfare agencies to wield over their clients, nor an appreciation of the coercive aspects of the casework relationship.

The limitations of the coalition strategy were clearly exposed in 1970 when the newly elected Tories refused to implement some of the key sections of the Act. Since 1968 the anti-welfarists have continued their case against the Act in a systematic and organised way. In 1978 the Tory Party committed itself to introduce radical changes in the Act, appealing, unlike the Labour Party, to various strands in the ideologies of working people (Hall, 1979).

What does this analysis of the Children and Young Persons Act mean for welfare workers in child care? First, and in line with our overall analysis, the policy which is actually experienced by welfare workers as a coherent whole is in fact the construction of very different conceptions of reality and social explanation. The Children and Young Persons Act is riven with central contradictions in the same way as is the Seebohm Report. It represents an attempt to come to some minor understanding of a different model of the causation of social behaviour. By introducing welfare, in a very limited way, into the legal framework of juvenile justice, it constructed an inevitable experience of confusion.

Why did this happen? Our characterisation of social democracy as a form of change is important here. We believe that, like Seebohm, this Act does represent an important advance, but one that was based upon such weak alliances that it *never* had power to take the full step forward. Let us be clear about the conception of politics used here. Legal change is brought about by getting sufficient MPs to vote for it; this is achieved by constructing a lobby of experts who can discuss the change in question in direct relation to some major political and social problem that MPs can understand. Here the Act was argued around 'reducing levels of delinquency'; this is something that MPs would see as important in terms of their electoral fears on 'law and order', and in the case of the Labour Party can link directly with their general welfarist belief. If we compare this with 1980, the only clear winning argument formed from such a politically weak coalition would be one based on massive custodial sentences for delinquency, the point we are making is that power and change are viewed in a very distinct way.

Change engineered on this basis by the left has no clear power base *either* in the ideologies of state representatives or in the lives of ordinary people. There are some direct parallels in welfare workers' attempts at change here. If social democratic welfare workers want to move something forward in the social service policy of a city or an area, it is most likely they will do this with as little reference to working-class organisations as possible. They would justify this for two reasons: first, such organisations are not interested; secondly, they represent ideologies which would be perceived as 'further to the right'. Therefore they would be by-passed as quietly as possible.

A number of consequences can be identified as a result. First, the proponents of change end up with *only* the power of argument to use in favour of change, a form of power which is weak and which can only wrest a very small part of the change that they want. Secondly, whenever there is a concerted attack from those in favour either of the *status quo* or of a more punitive position, there is then great difficulty in defending the reform. Thirdly, by constructing change in this way the actual operation of the change is left to state bureaucracy; it comes down from the top, in this case, to magistrates — and they operate it, at best, grudgingly. Fourthly, and most disastrously in the long term, by not engaging in such discussion with working people and their organisations we leave these opinions to be formed by the popular press and the media. This mode of change is shallow in its achievements, fragile in holding on to them and patronising to the working class. We see this as fitting the Children and Young Persons Act completely, and we believe that it explains why the progress made was so limited in implementation and why it has come under increasing attacks over the decade.

We would like to continue our analysis of the overall policy before we turn to the ideological and practical aspects of the legislation. There is a continuing debate about the nature and merits of the welfare and justice model of the state's relationship with statutory child care. First, given the failure to construct the full political coalition for change there is no reality in the claim that the welfare model has ever been fully put into effect. It is true that since the 1969 Act the welfare model has had some direct effect on the system; a system which no longer rests totally upon ideas of individual responsibility in justice. The welfare model contains within it some other forms of causal dynamic which we see as in conflict with the justice model of individual responsibility, of punishment and blame. However we would stress that both these models are at work at the moment and they are at work in an antagonistic way. There is also no doubt that the justice model is the dominant model both within the workings of the Act and within the social relations of the wider society. The welfare model will only become dominant with a struggle on a much wider basis than purely that of child care.

Secondly, we see the welfare model as progressive, and would argue against those of the right or the left who want to return to the pure justice model. It is true that for the most part the children prefer the justice model, but as we say in the next section, children themselves are comprehensively placed within dominant ideology. It is not that the justice model is in any clear way a positive choice for them; rather it is a model that appeals to ideological notions that children already have: the notion of 'fairness' under the law. That does not mean that children think it is right to get committed to detention centre for having a fight at a football match. It simply means that the justice model is congruent with the rest of the dominant ideology around them.

The problem with the pure justice model of blame and punishment — and we are surprised to find so many left-wing supporters for it — is that it contains a model of social causation which is quintessentially individualistic. In any form of progress towards a socialist society it is *essential* to move away from such ideology and practice. We see the welfare model as the first small step towards that objective in justice: it needs extension; it needs to contain a much stronger political base; it needs to contain a different understanding of what causes criminal behaviour. But it does represent one of the few moves in law away from individualism in causation.

PRACTICE, IDEOLOGY AND CHANGE

We have tried to outline the way in which the Children and Young Persons Act is a *constructed* form of law and policy. We do this to show how welfare workers work within and against certain forms of politically structured policy; we do it also to underline the fact that one of our prerequisites for change and movement is the involvement of all welfare workers in the reconstruction of such policies. There is no simple split between practising the Children and Young Persons Act and in fighting politically to change the law on child care. If we make that split then we simply reconstruct the social democratic forms of politics that leave politics up to the Cabinet and experts. It is necessary to engage a much wider set of class forces in moving forward. We now turn to looking at ideology because that represents yet another, though more hidden, constraint upon our practice.

HOW WE VIEW CHILDREN — THE IDEOLOGY OF CHILDHOOD

If there is one area of social work in which the full variety of responses to what are often very difficult and extremely confusing situations is to be seen then it is work with young people. Social work practice in relation to young people can at any one time be characterised in any number of ways: humanistic, repressive, disinterested, egalitarian, reassured or panic-stricken. We have spent some time analysing the history of the legislation and policy which directly contextualises practice with young people and in common with the other two areas of work examined (work within a social service department and community work) we would argue that the full explanation of social work with young people must focus on current practice. Unlike the other two areas of work examined we are in this discussion going to spend some time looking at the ideology that underpins much of this practice. In a sense it is unusual and some would argue unprofitable to separate out ideology from practice. We do so because many of the assumptions which underpin much of our work remain hidden or at least are expressed at the level of common sense. The precise effects and the ways in which these ideologies are expressed in practice can only we believe be fully identified if they are somehow singled out and examined in isolation. What we seek to show is that the views social workers have of young people are not only complex but are also made up of a series of different and often antagonistic aspects.

Dominating our view of childhood is the conception of it as a process of *maturation*; a period in which children and young people gradually learn the ways of adulthood; a period in which adults' treatment of children and young people is defined by their views as to the maturity or otherwise of a child or young person; a period in which by definition a child or young person is *deficient*. Now this is not necessarily a pejorative conception of young people. 'Growing up' does entail the development of a person emotionally, intellectually, physically and sexually, and is characterised by the movement from dependence to independence. It is a period of massive and often powerful change, the precise nature of which has been the subject of many studies. We wish to look at some of the views that flow from this central conception of childhood and adolescence.

In the interaction between children and adults what is often at 'stake' is the validity of the perceptions each has either of the other, or of certain actions or behaviour. An abiding experience of children and young people in these interchanges is that adults 'take no notice anyway', or 'just don't understand'. In other words the perceptions, views and feelings that children and in particular adolescents have of their world and themselves are not treated as legitimate but rather as distortions and illusions of reality which 's/he will grow out of'. It is not that adults consistently ignore children and young people: it is that their views of them and their behaviour in relationship to them are defined by the widespread assumption that young people cannot necessarily judge what is in their best interests. There are of course many occasions when this is obviously true. However, it is the consequences of these deep-seated views with which we are most conccerned here, in particular the role and status of children and young people in the decision-making that affects their lives, this being but one aspect, of obvious and direct relevance to social work, of the overall *subordinate* position within which children and young people carry out their lives. The objective elements of this subordinacy are to be found in an examination of the material, political and economic features of children and young peoples' lives. It is important to make the point here that it is not merely *age* which defines the nature of this subordinacy but the *class position* of a child or young person. However the subjective elements of the subordinacy which children and young people experience in their interactions with the adult world are much more difficult to lay out since they are subject to a variety of ideologies which can either reinforce subordinacy or sustain moves towards independence.

What we are pointing to is a situation in which children and young people do not have the *power* either socially, politically or economically to ensure that their views and opinions are accepted as legitimate and essential to any inter-action with the adult world. They have then, in carrying out their lives, either to rely on the ideological predisposition of adults towards them, or to seek from a subordinate position to negotiate in a whole variety of ways the outcome of any one particular situation. Many of the children and young people who come to the attention of social services and are defined by them and others as 'difficult' have learned that relying on adults is a tenuous and even sometimes physically dangerous way of operating. 'She's only a kid' one minute and 'wait till I get my hands on that little ————' the next.

We develop this analysis of *subordinacy* to show that the way in which we view children and young people, our ideo-logical predisposition, *directly* impacts upon their experience of *their* world, and informs much of our action towards them. With this in mind, and given that social workers are 'forced' by the nature of their work to seek to understand children and young people's behaviour and often, within the structures of child care, case conferences, courts, etc., to explain it, it is important to look at some of the assumptions that are made about children and young people.

We begin by examining notions about adolescence. Certainly most social workers accept this part of a young person's life as a period of significant change, biologically and emotionally. They accept in the classic formulation that it is a period in which more than at any other time young people are trying to work out their relationship to the world and are seeking to understand who they are themselves and what other people's opinions of them are. But it is also seen as a period to be 'got through' with as few problems as possible and a period during which there is a high risk of their coming to the attention of the social services.

Much of the work undertaken with adolescents assumes that the views and opinions of young people are the product of this period of transition and confusion. The legitimacy and importance afforded to the explanations young people give therefore are often limited, the explanations provided often being seen as peripheral to the social work process. The consequences of this situation can be alarming for it is precisely during this period that young people require their views to be considered and taken seriously, a testing of themselves often being carried out in their relationships with other people. On finding that the opportunity to do this is often not afforded in the social work situation the young person finds that his/ her withdrawal and non-engagement is labelled in a whole variety of pejorative ways. This is the experience of young people in their interaction with social workers: they are seen as being incapable of making valid and reasonable decisions. It does not however describe the full panoply of ideologies that are to be found in the 'social work response' to young people. It is not that social workers necessarily *want* to view young people sceptically, it is that in assuming that they are 'still growing up' social workers are *unsure* as to how much validity to ascribe to an adolescent's view of his/her world.

Another assumption that underlies many of our views in relationship to young people, which stems directly from the notions we have about adolescence, is that it is a phase that *all* kids go through. There is sound evidence to suppose that there are elements in this process which are common to all young people. But the overwhelming power of the ideology of adolescence is such that certain factors which differentiate one young person's experience from another's are often overlooked. It is more often the family background and home environment that is looked to to provide the information regarded as essential to a 'proper' social work response, than the experiences of the young person which after all, all kids go through! There are, of course, many times when we would want to argue that our assumptions with regard to young people are based on too individualistic a conception of them. What we have tried to show is that when social work provides an essentially individualised response the young person cannot guarantee that the ideological assumptions which inform that response are necessarily in his/her own interests.

Those elements of social work practice in which the control aspects of the work are visible demand that attention should be paid to the assumptions upon which they are based. The statutory requirements and duties that social workers have to undertake exhibit a clear contradiction in our views of children and adolescents. The essence of this contradiction hinges around the notion of 'protection'. For whilst there are obvious examples when it undoubtedly is the case that young people do require protection, it is in the whole argument with regard to the 'rights' young people have that our assumptions about their maturity — their ability to make valid decisions — make their full impact on our actions.

The debate that is emerging with regard to the rights that young people have, or should have, started fairly recently but is now in full cry. Later in this chapter we will discuss the way in which groups like 'Who Cares' (a group of young people in residential care) are playing a role in demanding their rights within care institutions; this raises crucial issues such as the role of children in their own case conferences.

Some of these rights are enshrined in documents such as the United Nations Charter on children's rights and are not wild or outlandish demands. We have included this section on ideology to demonstrate that such rights are contrary to the basic day-by-day assumptions we make about children. Overcoming them is one of the necessary movements in any progress in the direction of socialist child care.

STRUCTURES IN CHILD CARE

We have discussed what we have identified as certain important strands in the ideology of 'childhood' and adolescence. We now go on to discuss social service departments (SSDs) as a site where social work ideologies become concrete social practices. The SSD is the sum of the structures that actually concretise these ideologies, so there exists an intimate relationship between ideology/structure/practice/policy. This formulation identifies the structures as the link, the bridge between ideologies and practice. They are constructed by ideologies as techniques for achieving practice ends.

This contains an important idea; that structures are actually *constructed* not as the simple intentions of individuals but through political struggle. It follows from this that political struggle can deconstruct and reconstruct the structures within which we practice.

The basic and obvious structure is that of individual *casework*. It is not simply a form of practice but a structure supported and maintained by ideologies (individual practice, confidentiality, etc.) and concrete forms of practice (case files, home visits, interviews, etc.). This structure has an intimate relationship to forms of class struggle. Casework originated as a form of intervention in the lives of the poor which related to 'moralising' the poor through the selective use of material and spiritual guidance (Jones, 1978). It attempted to save the deserving poor and simultaneously to condemn the undeserving. This construction contained within it certain features which now allow social workers to maintain areas of practice shielded from direct management intervention. This area is actively constructed by bourgeois concepts of privacy, professional autonomy and confidentiality. Thus an area in social work practice is maintained which belongs almost exclusively to the social worker and the client. Management/state control can only be achieved in these areas by strong indirect means (supervision, resource allocation). This is the structure that allows 'professional sabatours and middle class bandits' (Pearson, 1975) to exist. Hence, whilst this autonomous arena was constructed by bourgeois values in the nineteenth century it does contain some important vestiges of the freedom to work in a different way.

The area of *professional expertise* has been extended and defended by social workers. We have outlined the way in which Seebohm has interacted with these values and ideas, but we have also outlined the way in which this freedom to interact with clients is under attack. This comes from computerised records, deskilling, disciplining, etc. It is the space created within that relationship that allows any different form of *direct* interaction with clients to occur. This is one clear reason why social service department welfare workers can be seen as the direct allies of working people as against the way in which the rent collector and the social security clerk are experienced by working people.

The state finds the casework relationship 'functional' as long as the state agent remains defined by dominant social practices. However, in recent years the state has had considerable problems in reproducing its agents. We have already pointed out the effects of trade union consciousness and to this we would add the beginnings of a penetration of Marxist ideas into social work ideologies. These developments have confronted social work management with a direct problem compounded precisely by the casework relationship that they had previously depended upon. The very privacy of that relationship allows the social worker to practice outside dominant state ideologies. This allows the progressive struggle for different forms of welfare intervention to be worked out in detail.

The idea of looking at, and understanding, taken-for-granted concepts helps us in our practice in child care, since it allows us to question such structures as 'case conferences', 'allocation', 'supervision' and 'reviews'.

If we examine the concept of 'allocation' we can see that it contains a number of crucial points — the identification of problems, the individualisation of problems, the distribution by a 'superior' worker of the work on these problems to (inferior) case workers who take responsibility for them.

In an obvious way then allocation represents certain power relationships which direct certain forms of practice relationships. In some social service departments there are attempts to struggle for 'open' allocation meetings, where the identification of these problems becomes a collective decision, where team members are allowed to look in a wider fashion at the social problems in their locality. This allows us to look at the relationship to these problems in a shared way. Such a collective approach challenges the hierarchical distribution of work and the idea of individual responsibility as well as beginning to restructure the overall relationship to the area. Yet this is usually seen as a simple 'technical' process of how work becomes allocated, and whilst we are not suggesting that open allocation will revolutionise welfare work we do see that it can play an important role in the general increase of democratic involvement.

Similarly it is important that such struggles take place over practices such as supervision and case conferences. All such structures contain major elements of contradiction between hierarchy and democracy. Here we are underlining the importance of the general increase in democratic possibilities.

CHILD CARE PRACTICE

Thus far we have tried to show the way in which the structures of child care decisions take place within a context that is subject to important contradictions at the level of policy formulation and also in their implementation. Whilst such a context imposes a whole range of limits and possibilities it does not totally determine practice: within parameters change can be wrought in practice in such a way as to ensure a general attack upon those wider parameters in the future.

One of the greatest sources of disquiet amongst social workers derives from their power to remove children against their will and against their parents' will. We wish to examine that arena of practice as perhaps the one where the practice possibilities are seen to be heavily limited by the state.

Powers are available to receive children into care when they are deemed not to be receiving 'care and control' and where this is unlikely to be provided if they remain with their parents. The aim of this provision is to protect children who do not seem to be getting 'proper care'. The state here idealises the family as being capable of fulfilling certain functions and it then attempts to reform those families that do not fulfil these functions. If this reform (preventative work) fails, then social workers can begin care proceedings. It should be clear that the social worker cannot go into this situation as an objective judge of the situation. The social worker goes into it as a state agent and with specific legal responsibilities. Equally, this does not mean that all room for manoeuvre is structured out of the situation. The very privatised nature of the social work interview means that the courses of action are not laid down in detail. We need to understand and work on the space that exists.

We see the contradictions that exist around the issues of care and control as the key to analysis here. We will also explore how children in care themselves experience social workers as having problems with their relationship with the child. The obvious central contradiction here is that simultaneously social workers are supposed to build caring and close relationships with the children, but also may be called upon say, to, place the child in a community school against their wishes. This situation leads to contradictory demands being put upon the worker which are difficult to handle. Here we want to look at the strategies that social workers use in dealing with these contradictory demands.

One way of dealing with this anxiety is through a tactic of distancing oneself. This arises from the contradictory position of having to enforce unpopular decisions on children with whom one may be required to build a close relationship. The distance, so advised by professional commentators, is constructed to allow the worker to carry out these harsh instructions. The problem with this coping mechanism is that it leaves the child isolated. It also makes it almost impossible for the child to relate to the social worker. The child may condemn the worker as uncaring since the relationship is structured over such a distance. Such difficulties make any constructive work with the child very hard.

The other tactic which is frequently adopted in coming to terms with the 'care and control' contradiction is by allying oneself as closely as possible with the child. This attempt to reduce the distance between the worker and the child under-emphasises the real power that the social worker has over the interaction. In building a relationship based upon a false equality, they gain some real trust. However the objective inequalities emerge at some point and when, for example the social worker has to apply for an 'unruly certificate' or a community school place, the child is left feeling bewildered and betrayed. It is clear that these two approaches reflect the contradictions of the position but do so in a totally inadequate way. The problem is that both approaches reproduce the constant experience of the child in care — that of being the object of other people's actions. The key to developing a progressive child care practice and policy lies in allowing children in care and under supervision some democratic and collective experience of the situation in which they find themselves.

This leap cannot be made totally within the casework relationship. But it will start with delineating the nature of power, control and decision-making that are contained within that relationship. The only way in which such individual gains could be consolidated would be by the connections made between individuals and collectivities. The idea of children acting collectively in anything but·play is a strange one to many of us. To those of us in any authority it is also very threatening, as the relationship between the teachers' unions and their fellow trade unionists in the National Union of School Students (NUSS) makes clear. Here the teachers reacted primarily as teachers and not trade unionists. However as the NUSS points out, in common with many other client groups, children are beginning to organise.

In 1975 the National Childrens Bureau organised a day conference for children in residential care. Out of this has arisen a number of groups, most importantly the National Association of Young People in Care (NAYPC) which meet locally and elect delegates to regional or national meetings. They act as support groups for campaigns and have gained some important reforms from local authorities. They have been criticised as being initiated and attended by adults. Far from seeing this as a criticism we would see in this the possibility for opening up a real alliance between the worker and the client which does directly challenge the usual power relationships contained within casework.

Obviously there is far to go here. The movement is small both in numbers and in strength. But if the individual worker/ child relationships are to overcome the pitfalls we have discussed, such collectivisation is *essential*. For example, as long as a social worker can only represent the child's views at the review, this action represents an attempt to develop a caring and honest relationship, but crucially it reproduces the child's *dependence* on the social worker and *exclusion* from important structures. Equally it is no real advance in the worker–client relationship if workers were to win *on their own* the right for children to attend their reviews. Such a struggle must involve social workers but depends for its base upon organisations such as the NAYPC.

We have identified the basis for making gains in child care practice within the present structures of policy and casework. We have not seen either the form of practice or the policy as totally representing 'the repressive state apparatus'. It is these contradictions that make the argument and the feasibility of a democratic child care practice possible. The practice will have to develop and be won not only within the existing set of structures but also around demands concerning such issues as case conferences, order books, privacy, etc. These demands will not be won as long as social workers and children remain in an antagonistic position. The democratic alliance needs to be built up both within the individual relationship and outside it.

Crucial to this development is the struggle for children's rights. We see it as inevitable that all human rights are only gained through struggle, rather than being innate. The NAYPC struggle is a part of this since once such democracy is won it will be much harder for some social workers to manipulate children in supervision or for children's homes to be run without reference to the residents. Democratic rights will restructure these practices as surely as the present non-democracy creates subordinacy.

In the short run the social worker can move towards these experiences of democracy by sharing the realities of their situation. We believe that nearly all children in care would respond to an objective explanation of the role of the social worker and the law. They would appreciate that the social worker is actually near the bottom of a hierarchy and is constrained by law and would be obliged to take certain steps if certain circumstances arose. It is important that they are in possession of this information.

Equally the other half of the equation is crucial. The child needs to know and talk about the circumstances in which s/he came into care, and to understand that in a way that does not pathologise them. This can be achieved within the individual relationship as long as each partner understands the real position that the other is in. This conception challenges all forms of abstracted professionalism that the worker might undertake.

This movement can be started individually by social workers but can only be fully *realised* by the collective support of organisations, be they the NUSS, NAYPC, NALGO or the area team. The crucial element that differentiates our conception of a movement towards socialist welfare work from that of radical welfare work is that the former cannot be carried out by individuals alone. We would propose that although we work and live as individuals, the movement towards socialist child care, for example, can only take place by our individual work being placed within wider collectives and eventually within a working-class struggle itself.

WORKING WITH THE WORKING CLASS: WORKING WITH THE FAMILY

The working-class family has become the site at which many social interventions take place. Working-class parents are asked to bring children into the world and bring them up as 'normal', 'well-adjusted', 'law-abiding citizens'. When they fail they receive massive ideological and material criticism. If only *they* did their job better then there would be no football hooliganism, mugging and so on.

Many working-class parents are well aware of the expectations placed upon them. But they are also aware that many of these expectations are beyond their realisation. All welfare workers will be familiar with the parent on a run-down council estate asking how they can keep their children out of trouble. There is of course no answer, at least not in the field of parenting, beyond locking the children in the house all the time. The problems are much more obviously structural.

Consequently, and understandably, when the children of such parents are brought into care their parents act with mixed emotion from bewilderment and anger even to relief. The juvenile court is symbolic of parental powerlessness in the community – it is a ritualised reproduction of their general lack of power in society. This exclusion is continued throughout the experience of having a child in care. Once again the working-class experience of the welfare state is beyond their democratic control and in the hands of experts.

Parents are also in a directly contradictory position within the law and order debate. They are accused of failing to bring their children up properly and as a result their children are taken into care. At the same time, it is *their* meters that are broken into, *their* estates that suffer vandalism. Not surprisingly this has a devastating effect upon working-class communities, particularly those with a high degree of juvenile crime. It creates suspicion, distrust and individualisation. Parents argue that *their* kids should be let off this time, but that the kids down the road are the ones that should really be punished.

The crucial factor here is once more one of exclusion. Working-class parents are experiencing a number of situations being imposed upon them — estates are built, bus fares go up, a playground is shut, a youth club built or closed down, but rarely do these developments have any democratic relationship to the area in which they live. After this, the parents are then blamed for what goes on in the area. We would argue again that the growth of local direct and representative democracy and control is vital if working people are to develop a full understanding of such events. Such democracy is not a 'con' on working people; it must be developed if child care ideology and practice is to move forward in any way at all. Until this struggle grows, all state support and assistance offered to the working-class family will be bureaucratised and experienced as imposed.

This need also applies to child care practice and facilities. Ultimately community care means democratic control of facilities by the users and the locality. Again, these demands need to be built and the initial steps involve demanding parental rights at case conferences, the right to know if their child is on an 'at risk' register, and so on. Without such involvement there is no clear way that working people will defend these aspects of welfare from right-wing attacks.

We do not want to be seen as idealising working-class parenting. We would not deny that children sometimes need protection from their parents. We do however, want to see child care in Britain constructed in a democratic way thereby allowing the aspects of 'bad' parenting to come under some democratic and local discussion, rather than being left as a matter for bourgeois judges and individualised law.

The reader will have noticed that democracy has been the recurrent theme in this chapter. This may be a familiar concept when talking about local authorities, but we also see it as essential when discussing all levels of child care policy and practice. The key break with social democracy comes at the point of arguing for direct democratic involvement at the level of individual relationships with clients, at the level of collectives of clients and workers; at the level of ideology; and at the level of the direct involvement of the working class in the construction of a progressive child care policy.

5
Community Work – Restructuring State Relationships

Several years after the launching of the Community Development Project in 1969 the enthusiasm and optimism which greeted the advent of a new form of 'welfare' work in Britain — community work — might now be seen to have been somewhat misplaced. The claims of a rich diversity of projects purporting to enable groups of working-class people to exercise more control over their lives by actively campaigning on a collective basis around the issues affecting them are now treated more circumspectly. And only latterly has it become widely recognised amongst community workers that in common with *all* other forms of state 'welfare' work, community work is subject to the deep contradictions that sponsorship and control by the state brings. The caution reflected in these opening remarks is, we consider, essential given that we wish to address the long-standing question of what the limits and possibilities of a progressive form of community work practice may be. The necessity for caution is reinforced by the recognition that recently the community work field in Britain has changed very considerably and that the direction of this change has in the main been one of *retrenchment*.

The elements of the change that we identify below are in themselves not unknown to community workers and other state welfare workers. Given the wide variety of practice that has gone on under the label of 'community work' since the late 1960s what we present is a renewed emphasis on *certain features* in that practice alongside the decline of other parts.

First, the nature and conditions of the community work

posts have changed. The early tradition of state employed community workers working in neighbourhood project teams is being replaced. It is now more normally the case that community workers are employed in much *closer relationship* to major state welfare institutions, in particular local authority social departments, some of whom have employed full-time community workers for some time, and more recently local authorities' education departments. If it is in this way that the state now more normally employs full-time community workers, there is also a trend towards employing people who whilst they are called community workers, work to a job description that is specific to only part of the community work brief in any particular area. For example, workers who are employed by education departments to work *specifically* with immigrant parents and children, or in the provision of adult education; by new town authorities to provide a reception and resettlement service, and by social service departments in planning and housing action areas. All of this work has come to be defined as community work and undertaken by 'community workers with special responsibility for . . . ' Alongside these changes *and* the decrease in the number of full-time community work posts available, there has however been a significant growth in the number of posts in which some responsibility for community work is either defined as part of a job or permissible within it — a *part-time* element within a full-time post. Here we are thinking in particular of teachers within community schools and social workers involved in such things as welfare rights and certain forms of group work.

These changes in the nature and conditions of 'community work' posts, hinging as they do around the twin processes of redefinition and dilution, form a central part of the overall retrenchment with regard to community work. They are linked however inextricably to the second major change which is discernable — a change in the essential character of community work practice in Britain.

Within community work in Britain there has always been a tradition of 'community development work'. Work in which community workers were involved in the stimulation and servicing of self-help groups, and in seeking to provide resources and facilities for these groups to function; a 'tradition' which has always been strong. An alternative definition of the work was developed within the CDPs and other community work projects as being concerned with community action and community politics. The change in the character of community work in Britain with which we are most concerned is one wherein much of what is now being done in the name of community work is 'community development work'. The retrenchment has meant the demise of one tradition in the work often actively pursued, for example, the closure of CDP, and the continued existence of another tradition aided by the processes of redefinition and dilution discussed above.

So far our comments have been made with regard to state funded community work, although they have some relevance to community work funded indirectly by the state through voluntary organisations such as the Community Projects Foundation and the Councils of Voluntary Social Service. However, the third major change which we wish to identify as having occurred in community work in this country is that there is now a recognisable sector of community work which is practised almost totally outside of the state's ambit. Not only outside the state's ambit, but also outside of its political problematic. Here we refer to the dozen or more independent or quasi-independent units which exist up and down the country, the most well known of which are to be found in Coventry, Leeds, Newcastle, Bristol and Southampton. For the purposes of this discussion two arguments are central. First, we would argue that they represent in large part the most progressive sector in both theory and practice of community work in Britain. This we would define by the relationship between the work undertaken by community activists and class politics and class struggle at both a local and regional level. Secondly their existence *outside* of the state is in part a function of the overall retrenchment of state community work to which we have pointed.

We have then identified three major elements of the change in community work in Britain. However, the changes in relation to state funded community work posts, the ascendancy of the community development work, and the existence *outside* the state of a fragile but developed progressive sector of the work, are the features of the current situation which must be laid out from the beginning if the limits and possibilities for the development of a progressive community work practice are to be discussed. In what follows we shall present what we consider to be the major reasons why what we have called a retrenchment on the part of the state and in relation to community work exists. This will allow us to discuss the limits and possibilities within a conception of community work which has significantly changed since the early 1970s and is now under threat.

We begin by discussing the origins of the community strategy in the 1960s in Britain. We argue that only by detailed reference to the process of the restructuring of both capital and the state (as discussed in Chapter 2), governed as it was by social democratic politics, will the rationale of a state inspired 'Community Strategy' and its major practice implication for community work be fully understood.

THE CONDITIONS WHICH GAVE RISE TO THE COMMUNITY STRATEGY: INNER-CITY AREAS AND THE CONSEQUENCE OF INDUSTRIAL CHANGE

In Chapter 2 the decline in the economic base in this country, particularly in the manufacturing sector was discussed; a decline that was hastened and became more readily indentifiable as the 1960s progressed. We identified the major elements of this continued crisis and its causes and most importantly we discussed at length the attempts by both capital and the state to regenerate British industry through the process of wide-scale restructuring. On the basis of this general analysis it is now possible to show a *local* level in which both the continued economic decline — and the attendant attempts to restructure industry into increased levels of profitability and productivity — materially affected the conditions facing many working-class people, particularly in the older industrial and inner-city areas. By so doing the question of why the state adopted the 'community strategy' *at that time* will be partially answered and indeed some of the major arguments as to why the state adopted the 'strategy' at all will begin to emerge.

The consequences of the decline in Britain's industry were most keenly felt in the older industrial and inner-city areas, and though the effects of this rapid industrial change were not confined exclusively to these areas it was they that suffered disproportionately. In particular the restructuring of industry had dire consequences for the working-class people who lived and worked in these areas.

A major feature of the industrial change as it affected these inner-city areas was that 'the centre of gravity of new industrial growth switches fairly decisively in favour of those areas which the government had designated for expansion' (Eversely, 1972). Manufacturing capital was beginning to recognise that real advantage in terms of space and labour lay outside the big cities. 'The older industrial areas saw little òf industry's new investment, for what new plant there was, was usually built on the outskirts of cities or in the new towns, where transport was good, and cheap land available for development and expansion' (CDP, 1977). However it was not only that *new* investment in manufacturing did not take place in the older industrial areas, but also that many of the *older* traditional firms operating in these areas were precisely those units for whom the economic decline was most severe. These features of the economic decline were common to greater or lesser extent to all inner-city areas which hitherto had formed the industrial heartland of Britain. Statistics bear evidence of the substantial decline in manufacturing employment in these older industrial areas. Between 1966—71 alone manufacturing employment in 'Manchester declined by 20%, in Liverpool by 19%, in Birmingham by 13%, in Newcastle by 11%, and in London by 18%. [The result] — unemployment in certain areas rose to between 10% and 15%. In Glyncornwg in 1968 . . . it touched 33%' (Community Development Project, 1977).

Another feature of the migration of industry from these areas which exacerbated their problems was that it was the technically more advanced and expanding industries that left for the new towns and growth regions. It was the firms 'that lacked capital credit-worthiness, and expansion prospects that [were] more likely to stay where they are. There are of course also the industries which are likely to employ a relatively higher proportion of older workers, unskilled women, and general labourers' (Eversely, 1972).

However the consequences of these processes on these areas did not stop at high levels of unemployment and having to travel, often out of the cities, to find work.

They are losing population, and the nature of the out migration stream is such that on the whole they are bound to lose more of those who are potential owner occupiers and fewer of those who look to the local authority for housing help. They are losing more of the relatively young, and more of the highly skilled or professionally qualified, and retaining more of the older people; more of the less skilled, the unsupported, and the 'problem' families. (Eversely, 1972)

The inner areas of large cities and the older industrial areas tended to become places with a much higher than average concentration of low income groups, including large numbers of immigrants, and a much higher than average level of unemployment, which has persisted in many areas throughout the 1970s especially amongst young people.

To compound the problems of these areas many were also experiencing a housing crisis reflecting a deterioration of the housing stock, a rapid decline in privately rented flats and rooms and increasingly high land and construction prices that put severe limits on new buildings. The long overdue response of the state to the housing crisis in these areas however caused further disruption for many working-class people living in below-standard accommodation. It was not until the passing of the 1969 and 1974 Housing Acts that the policy of slum clearance and redevelopment was replaced by the policy of improving existing stock. In the period up to this change in policy this meant that many people had to 'live through months of and sometimes even years of the blight and dereliction of a demolition area' (CDP/PEC, 1979), only to face the massive upheaval of being moved out of an area either to wait until new accommodation could be provided in the same area or to be moved to a new location completely.

This process of restructuring not only affected labour at the workplace but also and *at the same time* had severe consequences for life at home and in the locality. This restructuring of labour at work and at home was 'two sides of the same coin' — a process that in both its forms should be attributed primarily to the economic requirements of capital at that time. It is in this way that the existence and continued creation of the material conditions described above which many working-class people faced especially in the inner-city areas can be best understood. However the overall situation that developed in many of these areas not only had *material* but also *cultural* and *political* consequences.

A CAUSE FOR CONCERN

The material consequences for working-class life in these areas, as indicated by the high incidence of low incomes and indeed poverty, unemployment and poor housing and environmental conditions, meant that *concentrations* of 'deprivation' existed up and down the country *and* were visible. However, it was not only in this sense that these areas became a source of concern. The rising crime rate especially with regard to juvenile crime and delinquency was widely reported in both the press and official government publications — the Ingelby Report, 1960 and the White Paper *The Child, the Family and the Young Offender*. The demoralisation of the population in these areas when faced with the poor conditions in which they lived was exacerbated by problems of loneliness and isolation in a population in which many of those 'left behind' were the old and the poor. The particular problems associated with immigrant life, exploitation, discrimination and racism, were all the more evident in areas where a large immigrant population lived. Thus, at a time when the working class as a whole was the subject of constant and increasing change, the cultural cohesiveness of many working-class communities was being seriously threatened. A sense of 'decline in community' and alienation was beginning to emerge not only in these older areas but also on the new estates and in the high-rise blocks that appeared. The *political* consequences of this situation, as indicated by increasing industrial resistance, the race riots of Notting Hill Gate and later Liverpool, the growing disillusionment with established forms of political expression reflected in the low turnout of electors for local government elections, were becoming all too clear.

From being a material problem for many working-class people and their day-to-day experience of poverty and poor conditions, this situation and its political and cultural consequences became a problem for the state. The problems and deterioration of many inner-city areas in particular did not go unnoticed. The apparently small-scale isolated areas of special deprivation — overwhelming in the older cities — were a source of considerable concern in many of the government reports of the time (Milner Holland — Housing; Plowden — Education; Seebohm — Social Services; Skeffington — Planing). However, the form of the state concern, as we shall see, was structured around the ideology of social democracy. Therefore, concerned as it was with control and consent one of the prime modes of involvement was through the regeneration of the community itself. It was recognised that the destruction of that community, whilst it may have been necessary for private capital, destroyed the primary and popular method of social control, that exerted by the community itself.

Throughout the 1960s as the problems of these areas persisted in a concentrated and therefore conspicuous way the pressure for the state to react was mounting.

THE STATE RESPONDS — THE CONTRADICTIONS OF SOCIAL DEMOCRATIC COMMUNITY POLICY

We have suggested so far that due to the economic restructuring of capital and the consequent restructuring of labour itself, the 1960s was a period of massive dislocation within inner-city areas, a dislocation that had cultural and political consequences for the working class. This situation, as has been shown, became of increasing concern to the state, and it is in this context that the state was required to devise new forms of policy; forms of policy that *had* to relate *specifically* to the problems that had been created. Problems that were both persistent and politically charged.

We now turn to a discussion of the political and ideological imperatives of the state's response which taken together and explaining as they do the role of a *social democratic* state provide an explanation of why, along with other actions, the 'Community Strategy' was adopted.

The state was required to perform its basic but also inherently contradictory role. On the one hand it had to ensure the continuing profitability of private capital. On the other it had to deal with the consequences of the way in which capital operated and ensure that the working class could cope with these consequences within the boundaries of capitalist social relationships. During this period the practical consequences of the industrial change it was helping to promote had dire consequences for the working class. 'New forms had to be devised to carry out the State's old role' (Cockburn, 1977). As Cockburn has very adroitly pointed out: 'it [was] hardly surprising that the state in its job of urban management, keeper of the class peace . . . [was] looking for new policies and above all for new styles of making and implementing policies'(Cockburn, 1977).

These new styles of making and implementing policies were however governed by social democratic politics, since one of the costs of social democracy for the capitalist state in Britain is that the working class, operating as it does within that ideology, feels that the major social problems of capitalism are solvable. Consequently whilst it does not look to socialism to solve its problems it does look towards the capitalist state to do so. Therefore, given the obvious failures of the welfare aspects of the British state to solve the problems of class deprivation at a material and social level, it was of paramount importance for the state to operate as if it could continue to solve the problems of the working class. If the state were to fail in this respect, it would mean that sections of the working class would not necessarily be reproduced within the social relationships of capitalist social democracy. In the 1960s there was strong evidence that this was becoming the case,

since the indications were as we shall see that more and more
working-class people were withholding their consent, precisely
because the state was failing to 'solve' many of the material
consequences and social problems they faced. Social democracy was under threat and needed to re-establish *and* reformulate itself through new policy.

THE COMMUNITY STRATEGY

It is important to begin by emphasising that what was being
enacted was not just new *styles* of implementing policies but
a completely new strategy. A strategy that was inclusive of
many major institutions; as Cockburn has pointed out, what
was being proposed 'was not one or two isolated schemes but
[what] amounted to a movement involving several ministries,
many local authorities, consultants, universities, and voluntary
bodies' (Cockburn, 1977). It was a strategy that was to
deeply affect the fields of education, housing, planning,
social services, health and race relations, for at its core it had
a clear definition of the problem that the state, particularly
the local state, faced. This was the recognition that as the
local state in particular was being restructured it had been
organised into larger and larger administrative units and had
become more complex and seemingly more remote. The
more unintelligible the administrative machinery has become,
the less the working class felt politically linked to the state.
'This had created at least in local government a crisis of
legitimacy' (Corrigan, 1976), particularly a crisis for social
democracy. The 'solution' and a constant and important
theme within the community strategy was the necessity for a
more *responsive* government. It should not be forgotten
however that it was also a strategy that reflected the continuing economic crisis, the consequence of which was that 'more
aggressive problem solving [was sought but] within the
framework of reduced [public] expenditure' (Cockburn,
1977). This point will be more fully appreciated when the
way in which the strategy changed is discussed.

 If the community strategy was clearly developed to deal
with the material and social problems which many people

faced it was also a development which had certain ideological and political advantages for the state. The notion of 'community', whilst it has come to be seen as largely indefinable, was useful in so far as it did not state the problems in their *class* nature, for if it were a 'community problem' that existed, then the origins of the situation could be expected to lie within the actions and the lives of the people who made up those communities. As we shall see the consequence of the particular definitions that were used was to define the overall situation as a problem of people, of communities, rather than of industrial decline and change. However, if this was a dominant definition of the situation, it is important to explain that the different definitions of the problems that existed, which led in turn to the development of different forms of action, are all under the overall heading of the community strategy — a strategy which has been developing and changing right up to the present day. Before turning to the way in which definitions of the problems led to the development of a *particular* form of response — community work — it is worthwhile describing those parts of the community strategy which together with community work were constructed specifically to deal with the problems that arose in the inner city and older industrial areas. In so doing the *variety* and *changing* nature of the schemes will be noted.

1968 saw two not unconnected events; the first, Enoch Powell's 'Rivers of Blood' speech in Birmingham, the second the announcement of an Urban Aid Programme. This programme was 'to provide for the care of our citizens who live in the poorest and most overcrowded parts of our cities and towns. It is intended to arrest, in so far as it is possible by financial means, and reverse the downward spiral which affects so many of these areas. There is a deadly quagmire of need and apathy' (Callaghan, 1968). Many local authorities and voluntary organisations applied under this scheme for special grants to fund projects of all kinds and pay the people to staff them — often community workers and youth workers. Up until 1977, £43.5 million's worth of a potential fund of £60 million to £65 million had been approved. During this time, however, there had been five times more applications made than those granted (CDP, 1977). Urban Aid was that part of the community strategy which to a greater or lesser extent did provide resources for areas of special need; there were other parts to the strategy which did not.

Although, as has been argued, the strategy as a whole was aimed at 'improving' the relationship between government and public, particular schemes that emerged were directly constructed around this need. Thus the idea of area management was described by Liverpool's Inner Area Study as 'an attempt to bring parts of the city's administration closer to the people it [was] designed to serve through the actions of elected members and officials working within a formal area management structure' (Liverpool's Inner Area Study, 1976). Whilst one of the aims that the DES had for its Neighbourhood Councils was 'to represent to operational organisations (central and local government, firms with factories in the area etc.), the needs and wishes of the local community' (DES Circular LG4/743/43). In the education field the urgency of this problem of 'distant' relationships between in this case parents and schools was noted in the Plowden Report. Establishing Educational Priority Areas on the basis of the necessity for positive discrimination, Plowden's recommendations promised increased resources for schools in 'deprived' areas *and* proposed a much greater involvement of 'the local community' in the primary education of its children. In so doing, the foundations for the many community schools and community colleges that have since been established throughout the country were laid. Community schools were to be the medium through which the relationship between those providing education locally and local people was to be restructured.

This account needs to recall a number of other initiatives that formed part of the community strategy even if it would be laborious to describe each in turn, for they do reflect the changing nature of the strategy as a whole. The 'total approach' initiatives, Neighbourhood Schemes 1971, Management Guidelines Studies and Inner Area Studies 1972 were distinctive in so far as they aimed to cure poverty by concentrating resources of many different kinds on a small area. However these initiatives were to be superseded in 1974 by the Home Office-launched Comprehensive Community

Programmes (CCP). In the early 1970s *as the economic crisis worsened* the thinking behind the community strategy changed. 'It [was] not a question of providing extra money on top of existing programmes. The real question [was] to find within existing programmes the right order of priority so that money is spent in urban areas of acute need rather than in other areas . . . ' (Lyon, 1974).

The Urban Deprivation Unit extended this line of thinking, and the establishment of the CCP marked a clear change of emphasis in the community strategy.

> The problems of urban deprivation are such that they cannot be tackled effectively by compensatory programmes of the selfhelp or community developed type, or by particular innovative or experimental projects such as those financed under the Urban Aid Programme, or even by pumping large amounts of new money into small areas through environmental or physical improvement schemes... There is, therefore, no short cut to dealing with urban deprivation.
>
> The strategy [CCP] . . . is based on the proposition that what is required is to direct the major programmes and policies of government to those most in need. Decisions about the allocation of scarce resources must obviously be settled through the political process, but *new administrative arrangements can help to ensure that the political commitments are translated into effective action.* (Urban Deprivation Unit, 1975, our emphasis)

The CCP was to be essentially a management orientated scheme, a 'new administrative arrangement', an integral part of the local authority's budgeting and decision-making cycle, corporate management system and committee machinery. Thus, real solutions were seen to lie not in the realm of politics nor in the provision of extra resources but in improving administrative practice with modern techniques.

Finally another in the long list of schemes now in operation is the Inner Area Partnership Schemes. However unsurprising their appearance, it is significant in so far as they are a reflection of 'a major reversal in planning policy, [in which] the country's development resources will now be directed toward inner city areas' (Shore, 1976), in yet another attempt to arrest their economic decline. The views held in the urban deprivation unit in 1974 had taken root and as a consequence the Labour government's document of 1976, *Policy for Inner Cities*, appeared. Again the shift in thinking is marked: now, alongside the self-help and community development approaches, the management orientated schemes are in disfavour; the 'new solution' is the provision of resources through a partnership between local and central government. For the first time the problems in the inner cities have been officially explained, albeit if only partially, as consequences of the economic decline.

We have in this section both intensified and discussed those parts of the community strategy of particular relevance to the inner-city areas. It has been shown that schemes which provided direct resources to these areas — in particular Urban Aid — have run alongside schemes which have sought solutions to the problems by advancing better management techniques and administrative arrangements. We have noted an increasing disenchantment with these earlier schemes which have been replaced by attempts to deal with the problems at their causal point — economic decline. A change in policy has occurred which we will see, when we return to the discussion of the retrenchment with regard to community work, to be very significant.

COMMUNITY WORK — A STATE-SPONSORED ACTIVITY

In the previous pages we have detailed the origins of the community strategy and shown some of the elements in it. As a strategy it could not *simply* be an ideological charade. We stress this point because there are explanations of these policies that see them purely as a device to stop the working class from seeing the real nature of their class problems. We disagree with this explanation because of the material contradictions within social democracy. It was necessary for the policy to have a series of *direct* and *real* relationships with working people. Under social democracy these real material problems had to be addressed. Why though did these contradictions work themselves out within the form of establishment and funding of community work?

The notion that given the problems that exist in the inner-city areas the state was in some way forced to act is too simplistic. We have shown *theoretically* in our discussion with regard to social democracy the overall ideological precondition that prompted action. But the particularities of the form of action that emerges are always *mediated* by established patterns of thinking and acting. In the discussion of the community strategy a consistent theme that we referred to was the way in which the worsening economic crisis *changed* the nature of the strategy that developed. Similarly the *form* that community work took (indeed the *diversity* and *variety* or practice that has been called community work) was in the first instance directly influenced by the state's ideological explanations of the overall situation applying in the inner cities. It is important to show the way in which community work was mediated through these explanations and problem definitions which we will show to have had a direct bearing on the form of practice that emerged.

For a long time a continuing theme in the state's definition of these problems was that in fact only a *minority* of people were affected by them. Thus, the Home Office in launching its new Community Development Project explained that the scheme was based 'on a recognition that although Social Services cater reasonably well for the majority, they were less effective for a *minority*, who are caught in a chain reaction of related problems' (Home Office, 1969, our emphasis). Not only was it a minority of people, but as report after report substantiated, these people invariably lived in small-scale isolated areas of 'special deprivation and special social need'. These explanations had the benefit of confining the problems. They allowed for no recognition of *widespread* consequences of economic and industrial decline as they affected the working class in general. As a consequence the funds available, particularly in the case of Urban Aid, were attached quite specifically to 'areas of deprivation', the definition of which changed as funds became less available resulting in only areas of *special* deprivation being considered.

The dominance of this explanation was an important reason for the locally based nature of many of the community work projects that the state set up or sponsored. In the same press release mentioned above the specific intention of the Home Office became clear — CDP was to be 'a *neighbourhood* based experiment'. In the first place then, the extent of community work in Britain was in large part prescribed by the definitions which hinged on a *confined* conception of the problems that existed.

What is equally important however is to examine the state's developing explanation of why these social and material problems had appeared at their most severe in these areas. For although the major cause of poverty during the 1960s was the decline in the economic base, few of the early parts of the community strategy mentioned this fact. 'Instead poverty was called deprivation. It became a problem of people not of industrial change' (Community Development Project, 1977). A problem that was confined as we have seen to a few small areas in certain cities. The people who were of most concern were 'typically' suffering from 'ill-health, financial difficulties, children suffering from deprivation — consequent delinquency — inability of children to adjust to adult life — unstable marriages — emotional problems'. Pathological explanations of this kind were not only used in this connection. They have a long history and found their most secure home in the theory and practice of social work. Though they have been under considerable attack in recent years, in the early 1970s they found a new champion in Keith Joseph. It became important to utilise the same sorts of argument to explain the existence of *groups* and *concentrations* of people *all* 'suffering' similar problems. What had apparently happened was that they had become 'multiply deprived', whole families had become caught in 'a cycle of deprivation', that was not only 'transmitted from generation to generation' like some hereditary disease, but was also immune to the widely canvassed cure of 'equal opportunity'. Whole areas became affected, suffering from the 'social malaise' of 'urban deprivation' (Community Development Project, 1977).

Explanations of this sort, focusing on apparent deprivation and disadvantage, became the common currency of politicians,

civil servants and practitioners alike. A central issue contained
in these explanations was that of social control, especially
given the extent of the social problems, in particular crime if
not moral disintegration, that existed in these areas. It is
worth quoting two views of CDP. The first from a representative of the Home Office, the second an academic view from
Oxford University. 'In both the British and American plans
there appears to be an element of looking for *a new method
of social control* . . . [this is] . . . clearly a component in the
planning of CDP and model cities' (our emphasis). And 'in
other words one of the aims . . . [of CDP] . . . was to prove
that there was *an alternative to imposed controls as a solution
to social problems*' (HMSO, 1970, our emphasis). This view
of community work as being concerned with organising the
community, and stimulating self-help must in part be seen as
a reflection of the necessity, as the state saw it, of re-establish-
ing community social control within these areas. Indeed one
of the five main components of CDP identified by the Home
Office in the initial brief was the 'stimulation of local residents
to take responsibility'. Whatever the ways in which community work has developed, and often this has been in reaction to
this intention, the purposes of the work as defined by the
necessity for the promotion of community control must be
recognised.

Community workers however were not employed merely
in this capacity of control; another major concern of the
state was the importance of a detailed *knowledge* about the
areas and the people who lived in them. It should be remembered that the local state, in Cockburn's words, had been
'geared to govern' by the restructuring process to which it
had been subject. The relationship between community
workers, in particular CDPs, and the corporate management
system was carefully constructed. The intention was for the
CDPs to act very much in harmony with the local state's
management system. Not only in the provision of knowledge
through the action research components that were built into
the structure of each project but also as traffickers of
information *between* local residents and local state managers.

We have shown that community work, at least in its

initial forms was specifically related to the dominant analysis used by the state to explain certain practical problems. Consequently, neighbourhood based project teams, with action research components formed the basis of the CDP and many other community work initiatives.

There is however a discussion of the form that community work took which is not predicated upon an understanding of the dominant explanations that the state developed. It explains its form as being constructed within a central problematic for a social democratic state — its relationship with the working class.

It will be recalled that a crucial consideration for the state in adopting the community strategy revolves around the issue of 'consent'. The argument that it had become increasingly evident that many working-class people, particularly those living in the inner-city areas, were withholding their consent is to be found in much of the state literature surrounding the adoption of the community strategy. In short the *relationship* between the state and many working-class people had become both distant and fractured. Furthermore it had become increasingly the case that the *orthodox* methods whereby the state structures its relationship with working-class people had become seemingly less and less effective.

Given the low turnout of electors at local elections and the use made of local councillors, representative democracy at the grass roots could no longer be claimed to be a widely used and effective channel of communication. At the same time the mainstream state agencies of education, housing, planning and social services were also experiencing major difficulties in dealing with working-class life.

For a *social democratic* state the necessity for a *credible* relationship between it and the working class is of major importance. Without it the working class could not be accommodated to the consequences of industrial change *within* the boundaries of capitalist social relationships. Whilst it cannot be said that the state is *constantly* and unremittingly seeking to establish such a relationship with the working class, in the period under discussion, with the conditions that prevailed, the necessity to seek such a relationship was crucial. Without a clear understanding of the centrality of this argument to the politics of social democracy the emergence of the community strategy will remain either not fully explained or merely a *device* employed further to accommodate the working class to industrial and economic change and its consequences.

Such an argument does, however, have major and direct implications for an understanding of community work. If the state could have re-established its relationship with the working class simply through the existing and orthodox methods it would have done so. It is in this way that the full impact of Cockburn's argument of the necessity for *new* forms of making and implementing policies can be fully understood. Within this view, then, community work is constructed precisely within this central problematic for the social democratic state — its relationship with the working class. The terrain of community work is the 'distance' between the state and various working-class communities. In short community work represents a new method whereby the state can structure its relationship with the working class, at home and in the locality.

What is being argued is that the very existence of state community work is to a major extent a function of these fractured social democratic state relationships. However throughout this time the state at no stage dismantled the orthodox methods mentioned earlier. Rather community work and its move towards a more complex relationship with the working class marked a shift towards the limits of social democratic ideology and politics. For if the structural position of community work marked a recognition of serious problems experienced by social democracy, the community strategy and community work were *still* developed within its parameters.

As we have already pointed out, the attempt to create this new, richer relationship between class and state was to be no simple matter. Consequently the practical implementation of the community strategy *had* to have a certain 'room for manoeuvre' built into it. This meant that community workers were often presented with a wide brief, a brief that by the nature of the task had to include 'room for manoeuvre'. For if the policy was to work, and the job was to be possible, a genuine relationship with working-class communities had to be constructed.

It is important to note however that this 'room for manoeuvre' could be limited or expanded by the political considerations prevalent at any one time in any one place and as we shall see, successive moves towards its limitation have occurred in many places in the late 1970s.

We have taken time to state our position explicitly in this respect since it is central to our understanding of community work. If community work was to stimulate community activity and self-help, and to act in some ways as a state bridgehead, then of *necessity* community workers were required to build a close working relationship with the working-class people of the areas in which they worked. In so doing, however, we would argue that they could not employ methods which were entirely antagonistic to the working-class people of their areas. Consequently the 'community work method' has revolved centrally around organising rather than treating, and has focused on groups and collectives rather than individuals.

The remainder of this chapter will attempt an analysis of community work as it has developed. It will attempt to reflect and explain the diversity of practice that has been labelled community work and it will attempt to present a view of the ways in which community workers themselves challenged the brief with which the state presented them. It is in this way that the limits and the possibilities as expressed in changes in practice from 1969 onwards, together with the major problems and contradictions of the work, will begin to emerge. With an analysis of this kind it should then be possible to extend our understanding of what we have called 'retrenchment' with regard to community work. Finally the limits and possibilities of *current* practice in the *current* situation will be examined and the preconditions for a 'progressive' practice explored.

A VIEW OF THE DEVELOPMENT OF COMMUNITY WORK

We have explained the origins of recent community work in

this country be establishing it in the main as a state sponsored activity. It has been important to do so in order to distance ourselves from views which have presented community work in an unproblematic way as a 'radical alternative practice', a vehicle for 'significant social change.' Such views, though they are heard less often today, have often failed to address the deep contradictions that state sponsorship brings. However, by arguing that community work formed an integral part of the community strategy adopted by the state, and that its initial brief was consistent with the overall aims of that strategy, we have presented a *static* image of the work in which its functional aspects have been stressed. Whilst this form of analysis allows us to begin a discussion of practice which is underpinned by an account of the conditions which gave rise to community work, it does not explain the diversity of practice that has taken place. To do this, a different way of thinking about community work is needed, one in which what is stressed is not the state's definitions of the 'community work task' but those of the community workers themselves, not just a view of its initial development but rather the way in which it has changed over time.

Community workers have been employed by a variety of bodies and have worked in a wide variety of settings. No one body of opinion has been developed which has established a set of aims and methods which have come to be commonly shared by the majority of community workers employed at any one time, and whilst it may be possible to point to certain 'traditions' of community work that have emerged in the period since 1969, this is the case only because they have often stood in sharp antagonism to one another.

It will be remembered that our purpose in undertaking a review of practice is to clarify the limitations and possibilities of community work that has been practised in a 'progressive' manner. Within the diversity of practice that has been called community work then it is with one particular 'tradition', made up of those workers who have sought to extend their practice in a 'progressive' direction, with which we are most concerned. We recognise that approaching the development of community work in this way will provide no exhaustive study, but would argue that by taking what we will call 'progressive community work' as our theme, and by consistently seeking to define its nature and the directions it took, a clearer basis for the development of such practice in the present day will be made available.

It is the experiences of progressive community workers and the difficulties and problems that they faced from which we wish to learn. It is the ways in which they sought to change their practice as they met with these problems, with which we are most concerned. In short, we will attempt to chart a 'critical path' along which 'progressive community work' has developed in the intervening years since 1969, aware of the fact that in doing so we will inevitably distort a reality shaped by contradiction and riven with disagreement and confusion.

We start with the style that most characterised the community work of the late 1960s: self-help.

A DENIAL OF RESPONSIBILITY — SELF-HELP

The underlying aims [of community work] would be to create a more integrated community supported by services more integrated in their concepts and practices, and to take some of the load off of statutory agencies, by generating a fund of voluntary social welfare activities and mutual help amongst the individual, families and social groups in the neighbourhood, supported by the voluntary agencies providing services within it. It is therefore not expected that social action in an area will involve the provision of facilities which are individually large, expensive or wholly new in conception. [it] cannot for example hope to secure the provision of a new comprehensive school or the rehousing of a whole neighbourhood. Nor is it its purpose to do so. Large scale remedies belong to the steady evolution, as resources permit, of familiar policies. (Morrell, in Benington, 1974)

Voluntary effort and self-help have long been features of British welfare work. However, in the late 1960s they received renewed emphasis as twin methods whereby the problems of the inner city could be tackled. They became central, as the above quotation shows, to the aims and purposes of community work. And though, as a 'solution' to the persistent problems of inner-city areas, self-help has been largely discredited, it has not been completely discarded as a major plank of policy both within community work and right-wing social policy generally.

The proposals for self-help explained the *nature* of the problems in the inner city areas in a particular way. They utilised the language of pathology to describe families and people living in those areas and sought as we have shown earlier to confine these problems to a minority of people who were unable or unwilling to make use of the 'opportunities' through which the majority of working-class people had 'advanced'. It is also important to stress that underlying the rhetoric of self-help a particular explanation of the causes of poverty and deprivation was being advanced. *Given* that it was the social and psychological make-up of these communities that impaired their ability to function in a 'normal' way; it was with the people that the 'solution' should be most concerned. Hence the continued emphasis on the generation of community involvement and self-help as the means whereby the 'quagmire of apathy' could be broken and the regeneration of 'community spirit' and 'community pride' take place.

Within the context of reduced public expenditure the objectives were clear: a 'more integrated community' demanding no new facilities which were 'individually large' and posing 'fewer problems' with which the 'statutory agencies' had to deal. Following the victory of right-wing social democracy in all Labour Cabinets since 1964 this policy gained acceptance within all three major political parties. A policy which stressed that the responsibility for dealing with the 'problems' of life in inner-city areas was to be that of the working class communities involved rather than the state and its statutory agencies.

Rather than dwelling upon a more detailed analysis of the ideology of self-help, we now turn to the implications for the practice of community work. Morrell, 'the architect' of the CDPs, makes the relationship between this approach and community work quite clear in his statement above. Community work was presented by the state from the beginning not only with an indication as to the direction which the work should take but also with an analysis of the nature and causes of the problems with which it was to deal. A crucial element to any understanding of the development of community work is the way in which community workers have sought to establish different and conflicting explanations to those put forward by right-wing social democracy.

They came to question not only the modes and practices of community work but also the nature and causes of the social and material problems with which they had to deal. For instance, whilst it cannot be said that community workers were united in the understanding they developed as to the structural determinants of poverty and inequality, it cannot be denied that as a clearer and sharper analysis in this vein developed so too did the practice of a recognisable group of practitioners. This is an argument to which we will return as our discussion of practice develops. For the moment it is important to present a detailed discussion of a specific and inevitably complex and changing 'moment' in community work's history in which the ideology of self-help played an important role in the way it developed.

Much of the practice of community work at that time (indeed to this day) fell quite clearly within the guidelines presented by Morrell — the generation of 'voluntary social welfare activities and mutual help'. Other commentators have pointed to the widespread nature of what came to be called, in the language of community work, 'community development'. Specht, in his review of British community work, thought that 'much of what is now involved under the rubric of community work in the U.K. is much closer to what is considered in the United States to be social group work. In that it is concerned with strengthening and enhancing relationships amongst the members of a given collectivity' (Specht, 1975). Dearlove explained the continued existence of community development work by arguing that 'if community action groups urging demands for change and innovation in local authorities [did] not fold up [then often] their survival [was] maintained as the result of the downswing of demands, turning to self-help activities, developing a social welfare role, or involving themselves in assisting individuals to fit into and gain rights within the existing order' (Dearlove, 1974). The unavoidable conclusion is that, whilst what may be called the rhetoric of much of the community work of this time spoke of the aspirations for change that included 'increasing the awareness of the political and economic realities within which people lived' and enabling people 'to take more control over the issues which affected their lives', the reality in practice was a plethora of local community groups involved in the provision of facilities very often funded through urban aid, for play, youth in general, the elderly and later around such issues as welfare rights. Whilst we do not want to be seen as depreciating either work of this nature, or the activities of the community workers at the time, it is important to confirm that much of the actual practice was contained within this community development model. Nevertheless we would stress that whilst this work was going on a general process of politicisation of community workers was unfolding.

We begin our discussion of this by recalling our characterisation of the overall policy as containing inherent contradictions. Given these inherent contradictions there was no sure way in which the structure of their work could be set up to *ensure* that they would not develop different and alternative explanations of their work. Contained within practice were a set of experiences which directly contradicted the explanations of right-wing social democracy, for example, the *visibility* of widespread bad housing and dereliction, the evidence of years of neglect, poverty and unemployment. Increasingly community workers began to develop explanations at variance with those of the state which hinged around the identification of the structural determinants of the 'problems' faced. However, as more politicised conceptions of the work developed, so too did the analysis of the limitations of community work.

Community workers began to identify some of the contradictions of the work in which they were engaged. It became clear for instance that the problems of inner-city areas could not be solved by using the state's methods of self-help and voluntary effort, for 'many of the problems were not susceptible to solutions at the local level alone. Self help and com-

munity action within the neighbourhood may help to gain
marginal improvement and some compensatory provision but
the crucial determinants of the residents' quality of life
remained unaltered' (Benington, 1974).

In a short space of time the resolution of two major problems became the dominating concern amongst progressive
community workers. The first concerned the relation between
the theory and practice of the work. What were the implications for practice of a theory that located the causes of the
problems on which practice focused at a level far removed
from the locality and neighbourhood context of practically
all community work at that time? The second and related
question concerned the politics of community work. Given
the development of an analysis which was increasingly
presented in class terms and the continued, however unful-
filled, attempts to structure practice accordingly; was it
possible for community work operating along these lines to
remain a state sponsored activity whilst there was no widespread and powerful backing utilising a similar analysis in the
wider context of British politics?

For progressive community workers these have remained
dominating concerns from the first.

THE REALITIES OF REFORMISM

So far in our discussions we have been concerned in the main
with those parts of state policy which taken together we have
called the 'community strategy'. However one of the single
most important factors which shaped the way in which
community work developed from the late 1960s was the
implementation by the state of legislation and policy in the
areas of planning, housing and local government reorganisation. Taken together these policies changed the face of many
of our cities and in particular many of the working-class
areas within them, and formed part of the overall process of
restructuring to which we have pointed.

We would argue that fully to understand the policies it is
the contradictions within them that must be emphasised.
Quite clearly they were related to the long-term interests of

capital as contained within the overall restructuring of the economy. Furthermore they were the cause of massive disruption to many working-class peoples' lives, which was often exacerbated by years of delay and consequent insecurity as they fared either favourably or unfavourably in the decisions which determined public expenditure.

However to contain our understanding of them within the logic of the *necessity* for economic restructuring alone is to deny their very real *reformist* character. The complex array of housing—planning legislation to which we refer contained important initiatives which were constructed to deal with the widespread problems of poor housing conditions, dereliction and blight that characterised many parts of our cities. Some working-class housing *was* improved through the introduction of General Improvement Areas (GIAs) and Housing Action Areas (HAAs). And those elements of these policies which stressed the necessity for 'participation' and dialogue reflected the increasing concern of the state with the necessity for 'responsive' government and with the issue of consent. There is no doubt that we would concur with the criticisms that many, including community workers, have made in relation to these policies. They were *not* constructed specifically in the interests of the working class. They *were* piecemeal and often short-lived. They were, then, in the politics that constructed them and in the form they took, classically reformist.

We have spent some time discussing these policies and their nature because as we have indicated, we would argue that their emergence had a marked effect on the development of community work in this country. Through them the state intervened directly and extensively in many working-class areas. The housing and planning policies in particular became the focus of much of the community work that was undertaken. A common feature of much of this reformist legislation to which we refer was that when implemented it was geographically specific, for example, GIAs, HAAs and local plans, thereby reinforcing a community worker's relationship to a particular neighbourhood or neighbourhoods. Most important of all, however, is that as we have seen through an analysis of the contradictions contained within these policies, some of them contained the 'promise' of participation and dialogue as the means through which working-class interests might be mobilised. For some time the terrain of community work was dominated by the activities and policies of local state agencies as they affected working-class communities. Thus, alongside the practice that developed in relation to self-help community workers became involved in defensive and reactive struggles around issues that were in large part defined at least initially by state policy at either central or local level. What then were the forms of practice that were undertaken in relation to these policies?

Whilst we would argue that these policies represented opportunities for community groups to attempt to get working-class interests heard, this was by no means inevitably the case. But the evidence from the practice of community politics is that this could happen. The issue of participation, assuming as it does that through dialogue and communication between local state managers and community groups the interests of working-class people can affect policies, has been the subject of much discussion for those involved with community action. The argument that 'the complex of many pressures by which the local authority has been able to progressively transform the aims and functions of an externally constructed organisation with specific purposes and uses in order to ensure that it conforms to its own plans and needs' (Bonnier, 1972) has been central to this debate.

Given that community workers accepted the argument that these opportunities were not *merely* attempts at incorporation, in practice two ways of operating have seemed to be essential if the interests of working-class groups were to be influential.

The constituency of community work has to a very great extent been made up of local community groups, in particular the residents or tenants of a particular area or neighbourhood. As the receptacle of working-class interests, the organisation and effectiveness of these groups is crucial. For them to survive then it is their relationship to their areas or neighbourhoods and the people who live in them that will be their primary source of strength. The character of that relationship is political. For effective action to take place it cannot only *replicate* people's experience of representative democracy but also must seek to establish a state of direct democracy. This has entailed many groups in constantly seeking to establish a mandate from their constituencies, and most important of all, to establish methods whereby their constituents have some direct control over their aims, actions and activities. The importance of structuring a directly democratic relationship is to be most clearly seen at points of interaction with the local state, for the 'articulation of a majority view is necessary so as to restrict the ability of a local authority to act as an interpreter of the otherwise fragmented responses and potentially conflicting views of residents' (Benington, 1974).

Linked to this stand on direct democracy is the role played by individual community workers. Progressive community workers have constantly maintained that their relationship to their constituents is crucial and of central importance to their effectiveness. They have argued, often in the face of severe pressure from their employers, that they must be directly accountable to their constituency. They have attempted to ensure that the constituency can gain real access to the agency that employs them and that such attempts should be seen as a legitimate part of the *politics* of the work. It will be recalled that we have characterised state community work as having been created to work within the space between the state and the working class, a space constructed within particular contradictions of social democracy. Consequently they can be pulled in both ways, as John Benington has pointed out,

we came to feel that by the mere fact of our existence as an agency working within both the neighbourhood and the local authority we were in danger of acting in the role of buffer between the two, cushioning the impact of some issues. It was very difficult not to get into the position of the interpretor of the dialogue, and become the central channel of communication (Benington, 1974).

It is for this reason that we underline the importance of the relationship between worker and constituency in order to act against this constant state pressure both in terms of employment difficulties and problem definitions.

The perspective that we have developed within this section of the chapter has described the possibilities and effectiveness of community action as being bounded by what we have called the realities of reformism. We have stressed some of the difficulties community work faces. We have argued that, given the contradictions that exist within the reformist policies constructed by the state, and given the development in certain ways of the strategic relationships between the worker and his/her constituency and the community group and its constituency, community work need not inevitably be a means whereby working-class community groups are accommodated to the interests of the state. The argument remains, however, that community action provides working-class people with a collective experience which of itself is not a class experience, for in community politics the most important political category can so easily remain 'locality' rather than class. Community politics is of itself not class politics but a state sponsored activity which, whilst there is conflict built into it, is essentially localised and does not often have any regional or national form of organisation.

THE DEVELOPMENT OF A CLASS PERSPECTIVE WITHIN COMMUNITY WORK AND ITS CONSEQUENCES

In turning to a discussion of the development of a class perspective within community work we would want to link it initially with previous discussions of the different and varying explanations of the problems of working-class life in the inner areas of many cities.

A central cause of concern for progressive community workers in the early 1970s was that the work in which they were engaged had only resulted in what were often hard won but severely limited gains. This continuing problem of marginal impact and the increasing politicisation of a section of community work contributed significantly to the development of a class perspective within the work. 'Progressive community work' began to draw fully upon two major developments that were taking place in marxist theory in general. The first concerned an understanding of the political economy of localities. The second was a developing explanation of the role of the local state. We would suggest that their application to the struggles in which community workers were engaged gained impetus in the early 1970s and has continued to be a major influence in the development of 'progressive community work'.

The CDPs were in the forefront of this new analysis and the effect of these theoretical developments can be seen most clearly in the various project reports they have produced. In these reports, areas, localities and later cities were understood within the context of their historical development. In some, the historical development of both major classes locally has been stressed. In others, the specific ways in which the actions of capital aided by the state have deeply affected the histories of many working-class communities have been explained. These efforts to explain the *class* nature of many of the issues with which community workers were engaged provided the theoretical basis for a major development of practice; the attempts to relate community issues as class issues to the organised labour movement. The division between class politics at the workplace and in the locality has a long history within the British working-class movement. The strategy employed within this class perspective was aimed at overcoming existing divisions between community organisations, trade unions and other labour movement institutions. This was to be achieved by constructing joint campaigns and explaining within these campaigns the joint issues that affect working-class people at home and at work. This has led to an increase in city-wide campaigns and a movement away from the construction of small neighbourhood-based work.

The beginings of the development of this form of practice marked a decisive shift away from even the most liberal state administrator's view of the purposes of community work and greatly contributed to the eventual closure of the CDPs. Other factors which must be taken into account included the publication of a range of CDP reports which clearly exposed the socialist basis to much of their thinking. The closure of the CDPs had three important consequences for community work in Britain. First, it removed the only national community work organisation that was state funded *and* attempting 'progressive practice'. Secondly it provided strong evidence for those who argued that progressive community work informed by a class perspective and sponsored by the state was possible. Finally it contributed to the overall 'retrenchment' towards community work, which we shall now go on to re-examine, in so far as the 'value' of community work to local state managers was seen to be something which could not necessarily ensured.

THE RETRENCHMENT OF COMMUNITY WORK RE-EXAMINED

In the introduction to this chapter we described some of the features of what we termed *retrenchment* with regard to community work. We pointed to changes in the structure of employment of community workers and to the renewed emphasis on 'community development work' to the detriment of other traditions within the work. Before concluding with a discussion of the possibilities for 'progressive community work' within this current situation, this analysis of retrenchment needs to be extended.

We have consistently argued that it was essential for the state to allow community workers some form of 'room for manoeuvre' to develop their relationships with particular sections of the working class. We are now suggesting that this 'room' has been narrowed down quite specifically, given the situation in which jobs in community work are more likely to be found as a direct part of mainstream state agencies, in which their place in relationship to 'the management' is clearly established. As a consequence not only is it easier for these agencies to define the focus of work and to determine its objectives, but also the style and the manner in which the work is to be carried out can be more easily controlled. To exemplify this we quote from the instructions provided by a headmaster of a community college. The year is 1977:

1   It is to be clearly understood in your work with the
    community association that one of the guiding principles

upon which you operate is to establish a harmonious relationship with all members of the Board of Governors.

2   That as professional staff employed by the LEA you should not find yourself as part of professional duties in a position where you are advising, either verbally or in writing members of the community or the community association to take up a negative or destructive attitude to your employers.

The inference is crystal clear. The ability to enforce these instructions and so neutralise the actions of the workers concerned is in the first instance defined by the structural relationship between workers and their management. From this it can be seen that the range of issues or constituents to which the community worker can relate can now be quite directly and actively related to the overall purposes and objectives of the state agency in which he or she practises. Indeed particularly in the case of schools and community colleges the work of the community work team can often be quite clearly defined as aiding the service delivery of these institutions by acting as managers of plant and buildings. In these cases community workers have been literally 'captured' within the premises of major state institutions. The tendency to which we point is one wherein community work is reduced to little more than what in other circumstances may be called 'public relations'.

Finally given the current situation, both the politics and the ideology of 'Thatcherism' promise to have a marked effect on community work practice. At an ideological level the centrality of personal initiative and self-reliance to the Tory philosophy will seek to re-establish any community work within the ideology of self-help. Yet it cannot be claimed that even this limited perspective is central to 'Thatcherism', since its politics are not founded on the necessity to reconstruct a more credible relationship between the working class and the state.

STATE COMMUNITY WORK AND 'PROGRESSIVE PRACTICE' —
SOME CONCLUDING REMARKS
The diversity of practice that has been called community

work in Britain makes it impossible, or at least misleading, to talk of community work in a general and unspecific way, as if there were some central and unequivocal features of the work to be found in all forms of its practice. We have identified the tendency to view community work as a form of welfare practice that is somehow *inherently* 'radical and progressive'. This we reject, and in our concluding remarks we draw on the analysis presented so far to establish what basis there is to the view that community work within the state can be practised in a progressive manner. To do this we must return to that part of our analysis which concerns the structural position of community workers, most crucially their relationship to both the state and the working class.

Our argument has been that an understanding of community work begins with an understanding of the class contradictions within social democracy. In particular, the necessity to ensure that politically the working class are reproduced within the boundaries of capitalist social relationships. The relationship that this necessitates between the state and the working class can clearly take a number of forms and is mediated through the dominant ideology and politics of the time. At times when this is seriously threatened either by the withdrawal of the working class from it, or by other more *directed* forms of class struggle the social democratic state *is* required to seek its re-establishment. We have argued that the state in the 1960s and 1970s has attempted to do this by means of a 'community strategy' the central practice element of which has been community work. In part then community work was intended to reformulate the relationship between working class and state, *not* that this relationship was totally sundered but it became less certain. It had become increasingly obvious that the social democratic state was unable to solve many of the major problems of the working class, particularly in inner-city areas.

In constructing this new form of relationship the community worker had to be granted considerable 'room for manoeuvre' compared with other state workers, for it was the structures of these other services which had failed previously to cement this class/state relationship. It is this essential feature of community work that constructs any possibility for progressive practice. Indeed in many ways this 'room for manoeuvre' has only been fully revealed as containing possibilities, as the right wing of social democracy has moved to diminish it. We have described this movement in which the focus of the work is more narrowly defined and the day-to-day practice is more closely controlled as *retrenchment*. Under these circumstances, the possibilities for progressive practice have been *severely* limited and greatly reduced.

From this discussion of retrenchment it should be clear that this 'room for manoeuvre' cannot be guaranteed. In a general sense it is the politics of the way in which social democracy tries to resolve its contradictions that will determine the nature of this 'room for manoeuvre' at any one particular point in time. Specifically though, it is the way in which these politics are played out at the level of locality, within the local state and in relation to local class struggle, that will determine the precise outcome. Therefore whilst Thatcherite politics will seek to close down this 'room for manoeuvre' (quite literally in some cases), and in so doing not resolve the contradictions but merely deepen them; at the sharp end of the state's relationship with the working class, in the local state, the 'problems' will remain.

What we point to here is a set of forces which greatly determine the possibilities for progressive practice, but which are outside the control of community workers. The argument remains however, that the politics which the community worker brings to the state job and to the locality will also influence the way any possibilities for progressive practice will be seen and utilised.

The history of state community work practice can, as we have shown, be closely related to the development of a class perspective of the work. It is important to stress that this is not just a set of personal politics, but rather a theoretical and political framework which directly informs practice. We would see it as essential, in order to understand the very existence of the community worker's job, to have a clear analysis of the class nature of the key issues within a given locality, as well as the class structure within that locality. This would include a detailed consideration of the political economy of an area, the class organisations that exist, the divisions within them, their strengths and weaknesses and the overall way in which these forces articulate with the local state. In order to challenge right-wing social democratic definitions of the problems with which community work is to deal, it is necessary to develop alternative explanations from within this class perspective. From this standpoint it is possible to suggest certain features of a practice which might be termed 'progressive'.

Any form of community work must in part be judged by the issues which it takes up and works upon. The particular contribution that a class perspective would bring to this major and strategic set of decisions is to introduce important factors which are not related to the particularities of a certain locality. The stress on locality and 'community' is, as we have suggested, a state construct which can serve to mask the class nature of the issue in question. The form of practice that has come from his approach has often been essentially fragmentary and little removed from interest group politics. By remaining within these boundaries such work can only serve to increase the sectionalised nature of working-class consciousness.

The direction of a practice that can overcome these problems is one that takes as its major form the mounting of campaigns. The essential difference between this form of practice and others is in those people the community worker seeks to involve. In it, it is not just those who are directly and experientially affected by the issue in question or those of a particular locality to whom the worker addresses his or her efforts. It is necessary to involve a broader section of the working class not simply to provide more 'political muscle', but to broaden the consciousness of all away from seeing relevance *only* through direct experience. This approach is obviously not without its difficulties and dangers. If locality based community groups have a strength it stems from the immediate, material relationship the constituents have to the issue. A direct material relationship that can, if developed, contradict a subordinate and social democratic consciousness. However, a direct material relationship cannot of and by itself construct a political understanding which expands beyond the issue in question to a wider political perspective. Campaign work therefore requires that additional emphasis be given to what may be called the 'presentation of an issue' to a wider audience, if it is not merely and consistently to engage long-standing community activists.

For the state community worker another essential aspect of any progressive form of practice is the importance of developing direct democratic forms of struggle. This will make for particular tactical difficulties in the sometimes sharp relationship between representative democracy and direct democracy. In the past it has often been local councillors who have been the most vicious and vitrolic in their condemnation of community workers. Whilst the overall relationship of community work to the working class envisaged by the state was not necessarily clear, it was seen at all times to be essentially subordinate to 'existing channels', to orthodox political activity. For instance, the Home Office stressed in setting up one of the CDPs that it 'should involve no threat to existing channels of decision-making for the allocation of resources. In particular it aims to reinforce and not damage the spirit and efforts of elective local government.' The establishment of direct democracy is crucial to any progressive form of struggle since it is only through this form of organisation that working-class interests can both be mobilised *and* remain dominant in the carrying out of any particular campaign.

The obvious difficulty that a state community worker has in organising direct democratic campaigns whilst working for a state still structured around representative democracy leads us to the third major element in any progressive practice. This claims that any progressive community work practice from within the state will be proscribed by the relationship it has to working-class organisations *outside* of the state. Our central argument is that by itself community work cannot be a vehicle for successful working-class action. The politics of a class perspective are defined by notions of class struggle and class conflict. Community workers can assist this, and help workplace and locality organisations to understand and struggle around key issues *only* if the state community worker can sustain organisational relationships within which community, non-state organisations have some real power and influence. Only then can the skills and knowledge of the community worker be made available across the boundaries of the state to local working-class organisations. Again we would not want to underestimate the difficulties of this. The independent community work units that we discussed earlier, working outside of state control and therefore not subject to state imposed limitations, place this form of approach to working-class organisations at the centre of their work. They would be the first to admit the difficult and long-term nature of such work, even without state control of working conditions. The problems inherent in the work are those of overcoming decades of sectional consciousness; between sections of a workforce; between work and home struggles. For a state community worker though it is even more essential to work with such class organisations, since in the final analysis it is only through their struggle and 'progress' that the actual position of the progressive community worker can be maintained or extended.

We have identified what we would consider to be the major elements in any progressive form of community work practice and some of the difficulties associated with it. It will be noted that we have not defined how successful community action will be achieved in any one particular situation. To do so would be to ignore much of the analysis developed so far which has sought to explain the importance of factors outside of the community worker's control, which are determined by the balance of class forces at any one particular moment. What we have tried to do is to suggest the direction of a practice that will strengthen working-class organisation.

Finally, our analysis has shown the ways in which progressive practice from within the state is at the moment heavily constrained. Whilst we would argue that community work from within the state can and indeed on occasion has been practised in a progressive way, this is not inevitably the case.

6
Conclusions – Towards Social Welfare Work

We wish to begin by making a comment on the form of the book as we see it. Much of it rests on an uneasy tension between an analysis of state change, an analysis of practice and some prescriptions for future practice. In this sense it is to be distinguished from other books which provide an analysis *either* of the material policy context of welfare work *or* the forms of practice that exist. It is this separation that we have tried to overcome. A prescriptive work about practice often fails to root itself in the day-to-day material problems of the real situation. Equally an analytical work tries to provide an understanding which does not necessarily point to a clear form of activity. Our bridging of these two traditions is not an easy one; it does not represent a bridge of six lane highways from which practice flows to analysis and back again in a constant stream of traffic. We would contend that it is not just marxists who have problems in constructing this relationship; it is something that most bourgeois writers do not even attempt.

We have tried to write within this tension specifically in the three areas of team work involved in (i) social service departments, (ii) child care decisions and (iii) community work. In these areas we have shown the way in which a form of *work* can flow from an analysis of the organisations and policy that welfare workers operate within. All the way through, though, we have been careful about these prescriptions; trying to root them in what we see as a *direction* for socialist welfare work, but at the same time making sure that they have a base within the existing policy. This is not easy and many readers may feel that *at one and the same time* there is nothing new in the work since it is constructed by an analysis of present policy and practice, *and* that the prescriptions that exist are idealistic nonsense. Obviously both these statements cannot be equally true at once, but why should people feel that they are?

Welfare workers are looking for something different; yet they are also looking for something possible today. We are putting forward prescriptions for action which we hope grow out of the contradictions of social democracy. Therefore this can be *both* new and commonplace. Equally, we talk all the time of making a strategic stand upon these contradictions and pushing them as hard as possible and this may be read as idealistic. In this concluding chapter we want to outline why our prescriptions for going forward are not idealistic but have a firm base not only in the policy of social democracy but in the politics of socialist struggle both inside and outside the welfare apparatuses of the British capitalist state.

We feel it is possible to argue for this form of movement towards socialist welfare work because we are discussing *social democratic state apparatuses*. Even given the present policy of the Conservative Party we do not feel that it will be possible to shift the welfare state structures from within that social democratic framework for a considerable period of time. It is true that governments may try to do so and in fact make enormous inroads, but social democracy does have a real power over the hearts and minds of working people. They still expect some major welfare interventions in their lives and until this has been transformed we believe that the welfare state apparatuses therefore will remain a social democratic terrain.

We will return to Thatcherism later as it is of continuing importance as a political force and ideology and will be so right up to the full construction of socialism. Therefore, we rest our analysis on the contradictions contained within social democracy *not* as abstract forces but as a consequence of classes struggling. These class contradictions we would contend have a *direct and unremitting effect upon the possibilities of practice*. This does not mean that any of these services or institutions will *automatically* move in a socialist way. If we look at our chapter on state community work, it contains an analysis which sees the state increasing its control over the possibilities of progressive work. There has been movement to the right in our society in a wide range of ideological forces. This has affected all aspects of welfare but especially those connected with new forms of direct democracy; particularly those who are directly trying to link workplace struggles and home struggles from inside the state. This change has happened beyond the control of community workers. It is important to stress this here because throughout the book we have underlined the active part of the relationship between people and change. It must be understood that there are a wide range of social forces that we cannot *control*. We can affect them if we work in a broad democratic way, but we cannot control them.

The retrenchment we outline is emphasised to underline the fact that the institutions and struggles that we are discussing here are ones that are under constant pressures to change in the *opposite* direction from our own. We stress this to show that not everything is possible all the time; only specific forms of progress are possible at specific times. Here we will outline some of the general principles of work that we feel follow from our analysis and that can be seen as a movement *towards* socialist welfare work.

STRATEGY AND PERSPECTIVE – A PREREQUISITE FOR SOCIALIST WELFARE WORK

We must start with the notions of strategy and perspective. We stressed at the beginning that socialist social work can only be *achieved* fully with the transformation of all aspects of society; the mode of production, the relations of production, the state, everything. The struggle for this does not simply end with an event called 'the revolution'; as Mao points out (Mao Tse-tung, 1973), class struggle continues during the period of socialism. Socialist welfare work is something that will have to be struggled for and defended even when the mode of production is characterised by socialist forms.

We stress this because our book is about a series of political and practice *directions*, *not* about a set of institutional achievements. We are obviously not saying that this or that way of doing something is a socialist child care practice *within* a capitalist society. Unfortunately this may be what a number of readers wanted from the book and whilst apologising for disappointing them we would suggest that such an enterprise is absolutely impossible. Socialist work within a capitalist society is a matter of direction and not a matter of looking round the office and saying a particular part of my work is socialist and a particular part capitalist. We do not then help people out with simple descriptions of this or that practice with a particular client.

This is why we stress the necessity of strategy and perspective. If we cannot check on our practice *now* with some political socialist litmus paper then we need some way of making sense of our work. We would suggest that this cannot be done in a static way even though that may make us all feel better. It is necessary to look at the general and specific contradictions in situations and make sense of our input and action in relationship to the way in which these things move. It means putting today's work in the context of last week's, last year's, next week's, and next year's; trying to put ourselves into an historical process of change; trying to put our actions within that process. Such an activity of strategy and perspective is very hard but is an essential prerequisite for any socialist political movement.

We underline this point because there is no doubt that right-wing social democrats and Thatcherites *do* have a strategy for their political work. They fit their actions and behaviour into that; and whilst occasionally they get depressed about 'the rising tide of socialism' they have a class confidence in their actions which, we would suggest, most of us lack. And it is this that contains one of the major reasons for perspective and strategy. Without a sense of active history it is really very hard not to get enormously depressed at the world's intractability to change. If we don't put today's work in a past and future perspective it remains a unique and usually depressing entity. So, having internalised this idea of working with and on class contradictions, one can make sure that one's work and politics is placed within that perspective; a perspective for the future.

STATE CHANGE AND CLASS STRUGGLE

Having demonstrated that the *detail* of the organisations that we work for is constructed by class struggle that takes place inside and outside of the state, then we would stress the vital necessity of struggling in a co-ordinated way in both these arenas. Moving towards socialist welfare work means moving away from the conceptions of welfare practice that characterise the nature of social democratic welfare service.

It is obvious that we see welfare work as intrinsically political. Therefore we obviously reject the charge that when social workers engage in political practice they are introducing politics into their work. In 1980 this is an absurd charge. We contend that social democracy, because of the way in which it has related welfare work to political activity, has left welfare wide open to attacks from the right.

By trying to split political activity and welfare work, social democracy maintains for only a very few people the right to take part in political activity in welfare. The institutions and the organisations that right-wing social democracy have constructed have at all times kept day-to-day political action as far as possible *away* from the workers who work in them and the working-class people they serve. This has had *disastrous* consequences. First, it has led the vast majority of welfare workers to see themselves as totally separated from the year-by-year control of their work. This has led, more than anything else, to their frustration and depression. It has also impoverished the political processes of welfare immeasurably because the people involved have been removed. Secondly, it has led the vast majority of the population to see themselves as totally separated from the short-term, day-to-day and long-term, year-by-year control of the organisations of welfare.

The tendency has been for the welfare state in the late 1970s to be experienced by most people as external and bureaucratic. Over the last thirty years the accumulation of these experiences has turned significant sections of the population away from the welfare state as having any form of progressive role in their lives. Trying to get a council house window fixed, trying to get an Exceptional Needs Payment from the social security, having a chronic ailment and going to the National Health Service, going to the social services with any child care problem, going into schools to find out how the children are getting on, *all* of these are experiences which contain no element of democracy at all. For most working people they are humiliating and subordinate experiences. As long as this exists and continues, 'welfare' will *only* exist in a dangerous and precarious way. For it is absurd to expect that people who experience humiliation on a day-to-day basis at the hands of 'the welfare' will then turn round and defend it when 'the right' tries to dismantle it. In this way right-wing social democracy has managed to destroy any democratic relationships and feelings that existed for working people in relationship to welfare. These must be reconstructed.

DEMOCRATIC RECONSTRUCTION – A SOCIALIST STRATEGY

The basic site for this reconstruction is neither purely inside the state nor outside it. Instead it has to exist in the relationship between civil society and the state; it has to allow structures which encourage clients, workers and the rest of the working class to have a direct say. Therefore we stand not only for an increased politicisation of welfare work, but that it shall happen not simply amongst clients but in the way and the form that clients relate to welfare; an increased and extended democracy.

What, though, do we see as the elements of this democracy? First, that it should exist both at the structural level of *'the'* working class and *'the'* welfare, and the level of client—worker relationships; these *must* reinforce each other. As we saw in the chapter on child care policy, in terms of relationships with clients, with children and youth, most clients do not have very much in the way of democratic experience in their lives. Children at school, at home, and in fact all clients, have very few experiences that can be labelled as democratic. Consequently, it must be expected that they will treat any form of democratic structure or experience with deep caution; usually ignoring it as some strange idiosyncracy. This lack of democracy does not usually appear on social enquiry reports or on case notes but it structures people's lives most surely.

Therefore on a personal and individual level with clients it should not be surprising if many of them either ignore or hurl back offers of day-to-day involvement in solutions to their problems. This goes beyond the orthodox casework ideology of 'self-determination' since such a concept is an essentially individualistic bourgeois one. It is a nonsense to suggest that working-class individuals in the sort of capitalist society we have outlined in this book can really engage in determining their own activity in a self-directed way. Self-determination may just be possible for millionaires, but for a family on social security it frames the possibility of action in an absurd way. Yet we would suggest that welfare workers should engage with their clients in such a way as to increase the responsibility of the clients for their actions.

We have interpreted marxism in this book as a guide to action and not a cause for interpreting the impossibility of activity. A structural analysis of individually experienced problems can leave both welfare worker and client feeling, 'Oh well, I'm afraid its all down to the problems of the structure of capitalism.' The problem of democracy at the personal level lies in the sharing of an understanding and analysis. We have suggested that this analysis is based upon an understanding of contradictions not simply at the level of social relationships but in the organisations that welfare workers work for. Our analysis has stressed this part of the contradictions and we would suggest that it is vital for democracy to honestly share this analysis of the institutions we work for. We detail this in the child care chapter in relation to children; we try to show how this unpicks the capitalist ideology about children; how the policy of child care contains contradictions which must be explained honestly to the children involved and we show why and how workers achieve this.

Much of the empirical content of this book is about the move away from democracy that has taken place in state structures and we must remember the effect of this on people's experience of state welfare. People expect to be humiliated, to be passed from pillar to post, and although we see strong elements in the service that work to contradict this, our own activity must remember this base in people's lives. However, we would argue strongly against the social democratic position that clients are not experts either in their own or other people's lives; we would argue for their democratic involvement in as much welfare as possible; we would further argue that their exclusion from this process has laid welfare open for the attack from the right.

But democracy for us does not stop with the individual reaction of client and worker. It must take place in the relationship between office and community, between welfare workers and working class. We have tried to show that this must be fought for at a range of levels. We have also shown that, parallel to the individual level, it would be very difficult to destroy all traces of democracy both within the welfare apparatuses and within their relationship to the wider society. We are then, once more, talking about working upon a contradiction within these relationships; and we are not talking about the introduction of an idea or a notion outside of the normal run of things. Democracy as a word is familiar; as an experience it is strange for many people. But it is something which can be practically argued for at every level. In terms of the Seebohm constructed departments we tried to show the fact that they had to be built, in some part, on a relationship with the community, and a relationship around the team; contained within these structures there is an element of and a right to democracy. We know that such elements are continually under attack from hierarchy but would suggest that both between welfare workers and client and between welfare workers themselves it is possible to argue for greater democracy without putting yourself beyond the common ideology of fellow workers.

As we said, though, this commitment to democracy needs to be not simply a tactical one, one that is played around with or that takes place at elections once a year. Such a minimum commitment does not provide the secure basis for people to learn about their own practical democratic possibilities. If we look at the strike experience we outlined, or the relationship of child to worker, we try to get across the necessity for *structure* in the democratic experience. This is absolutely essential since we are all told all of the time that we 'live in a democracy', but few of us actually experience our world as that. This leads most of us to be extremely cynical about democracy. If we are to venture into the construction of democratic experiences and structures then we must make sure that both for workers and for clients they have a solid and enduring existence. We are suggesting that one of the reasons that the social worker strike activity had such an impact was the fact that it was a part of a set of institutions that had great historical and contemporary strength. Such experience of democracy is rare and needs fostering.

But what is the relationship between our strategic stand for democracy and socialist welfare work? We believe that the relationship between democratic welfare and socialism goes way beyond the interpersonal arena of practice or even the internal structure of departments, but expresses the vehicle best suited for the struggle for socialist politics and welfare. It is inextricably linked with the improvement of relationships, structure, politics, welfare policy and revolutionary change. We trust that this prescriptive political stand can be seen in our analysis of the changes in welfare state structures in Chapter 2. Here we identify the need for monopoly capital to shift labour about as much as is necessary; to break cultural and locality ties in the new state structures and to ensure that even the attentuated democracy of local government is diminished further. The overall aim of this is to sunder all effective political relationship between working-class organisations and aspects of the state. We go further and outline the way in which people who receive services are clientised and turned into passive recipients. If we believe that the only way in which socialism is to be constructed is with the involvement of the mass of working people then it becomes necessary to construct in a new and richer way the experience of active democracy and not passive clientism. The same goes for welfare workers themselves.

In three specific areas of struggle we have outlined the way in which we see this moving. We try to demonstrate the way in which democratic and collective struggle acts as the solid bridge between today's limited forms of work and the future welfare work under socialism. Here we want to discuss some of the wider political changes which will be necessary for any of this prescription to be at all possible.

CONTINUING THE WELFARE

As we conclude this work the day-to-day experience of welfare workers and their clients is dominated by the cuts in services and the restructuring that is taking place under Thatcher (Leonard, 1979). It may appear now more absurd that ever to discuss moves towards socialist welfare work, yet we would want to demonstrate that the *only* way that even a social democratic welfare apparatus will be able to survive is through forms of democratic political practice that we have outlined.

We have demonstrated that the way in which social democracy has constructed the relationship between welfare and the people has allowed right wingers like Thatcher to step in and build on this anti-state feeling. Consequently, fights against cuts are directly hampered by the experiences that people have of the services. In any sense the services are not experienced as 'ours'. We have suggested that this is related to the structures of state organisation contained within social democratic services; we suggest that it is essential in fighting the cuts and building welfare to ensure that the structures we are fighting *for* reflect the politics of that struggle. Thus, since it is only through widescale involvement of clients and working people that these services will be defended and extended then it is only through their involvement in the democratic experience and structure of these services that people will not turn again to an anti-state Thatcher. In the wake of the cuts many welfare workers are being forced into alliances with wider sections of the community. We have suggested that this has also happened within the experience of trade unionism. These alliances begin to replicate the relationship between work and politics that has been central to our book. It crosses the boundaries of state worker, worker, member of the working class, client; it is forced to form a broader alliance. We are arguing that the alliance must be built into not only the nature of struggle but also the actual experience of welfare work. Defending a service with someone as an equal must effect the way in which that person is treated when they walk into the office as a client; or the way in which the 'home' relates to the child. This then must go beyond experience into structure.

BUT WHAT HAS THIS TO DO WITH SOCIALISM?

One of the truths of marxism that we hold to is that capitalism contains within it the seeds of socialism. We have outlined how significant the working class has been to the construction and the continuation of welfare policy in the UK. We have also shown how any progressive movement in welfare work would need in the medium or long term to involve working people directly in it. The more that working people become involved in the construction and implementation of policy, in the actual experience of democracy in welfare, the more they build up a consciousness which reflects their ability to construct a social formation as a whole.

Now we are not saying that the welfare state is *the* central activity in building working-class confidence and moving towards socialism (though we would contend that it is *one* of the central arenas) but we are suggesting that the politics of this book goes beyond welfare workers. If welfare workers succeed in moving towards a socialist welfare work they can only do this by a direct relationship with working-class organisations. If they work with those organisations on developing the progressive and democratic involvement of working people then this in turn will build up the influence, confidence and power of the working class.

Bibliography

Abrams, M. (1965) *The Origins of Sociology* (Chicago University Press).

Althusser, L. (1970). 'Ideology and Ideological State Apparatuses', in *Lenin and Philosophy and Other Essays* (London: New Left Books).

Bailey, R. and Brake, M. (eds) (1975) *Radical Social Work* (London: Arnold).

Benington, J. (1974) 'Strategies for Change at Local Level — Some Reflections', in C. Jones and M. Mayo (eds), *Community Work One* (London: Routledge and Kegan Paul).

Benington, J. (1976) *Local Government becomes Big Business* (London: Community Development Project).

Bonnier, F. (1972) 'Les Pratiques des Associations de Quartier et les Processus de "Recuperation" ', *Espaces et Societies*, no. 6/4 (July/October).

Braverman, H. (1974) *Labour and Monopoly Capital* (New York: Monthly Review Press).

Callaghan, J. (1968) Quoted in Hansard, 2 December.

Clarke, J. (1979) 'Critical Sociology and Radical Social Work: Problems of Theory and Practice', in Parry, Rustin and Satyamurti (eds), *Social Work, Welfare and the State* (London: Arnold).

Cockburn, C. (1977) *The Local State: Management of Cities and People* (London: Pluto).

Cohen, S. (1971) (ed.), *Images of Deviance* (Harmondsworth: Penguin).

Community Development Project (1977) *Gilding the Ghetto* (London: CDP).

Community Development Project/PEC (1979) *The State and the Local Economy* (London: CDP).

Corrigan, Paul (1976) 'The Community Strategy, State Policy and Class Struggle 1966—1976', paper presented to the Fourth European Conference on Deviancy and Social Control, Vienna, September.

Corrigan, Paul (1980) 'Departmental Conference as Democratic Form', *Social Work Today*, 4 March.

Corrigan, Paul and Leonard, Peter (1978) *Social Work Practice under Capitalism* (London: Macmillan).

Corrigan, Philip (1980) *Capitalism, State Formation and Marxist Theory* (London: Quartet).

Corrigan, Philip (1981) *State Formation and Moral Regulation in England* (London: Macmillan). '

Corrigan, Philip and Corrigan, Val (1979) 'State Formation and Social Policy before 1871', in Parry *et al.* (1979).

Dearlove, J. (1974) 'The Control of Change and the Regulation of Community Action' in C. Jones and M. Mayo (eds), *Community Work One* (London: Routledge and Kegan Paul).

Donnison, D. (1968) 'Seebohm: the Report and its Implications', *Social Work* (UK) (October).

Donnison, D. and Chapman, G. (1975) *Social Administration and Policy Revisited* (London: Allen and Unwin).

Eversely, D. (1972) 'Old Cities, Falling Populations and Rising Costs', GLC Intelligence Unit, *Quarterly Journal*, no. 18.

Fryer, R. and Martin, G. (1971) *Redundancy and Paternalist Capitalism* (London: Allen and Unwin).

Ginsburg, N. (1979) *Class, Capital and Social Policy* (London: Macmillan).

Gough, I. (1979) *The Political Economy of the Welfare State* (London: Macmillan).

Gould, D. (1976) 'Measuring Social Work', *Municipal and Public Services Journal* (22 October).

Hall, P. (1976) *Reforming the Welfare* (London: Heinemann).

Hall, S. (1979) 'The Great Moving Right Show', *Marxism Today* (January).

Hall, S. *et al.* (1978) *Policing the Crisis* (London: Macmillan).

Handler, J. (1968) *The Coercive Child Care Officer* (Oxford University Press).

HMSO (1946) *Committee on the Care of Children, Report* (*Curtis Report*) Cmnd. 6922.

HMSO (1962a) *Board of Trade Journal.*

HMSO (1962b) *Board of Trade Gazette.*

HMSO (1963) *The Conditions of Faster Economic Growth* (London: NEDC).

HMSO (1965) *Children, Family and the Young Offender*, Cmnd. 3601.

HMSO (1967) Committee on the Management of Local Government, *Management of Local Government* (*Maud Peport*).

HMSO (1968) Committee on Local Authority and Allied Personal Social Services, *Report* (*Seebohm Report*) Cmnd. 3703.

HMSO (1969) *Children and Young Persons Act, 1969 — a Guide for Courts and Practitioners.* Part 1.

HMSO (1969) *Royal Commission on Local Government in England, Report (Redcliffe Maud Report)* Cmnd. 4040.

HMSO (1972) *Study Group on Local Authority Management Structures, the New Local Authorities' Management and Structure (Bains Report).*

Hobsbawn, E. (1965) *Industry and Empire* (Harmondsworth: Penguin).

Home Office (1969) Press release, 16 July.

Home Office (1970) Minutes of Ditchley Park Conference.

Hunt, A. (1977) (ed.) *Class and Class Structure* (London: Lawrence and Wishart).

Jones, C. (1978) *The Foundations of Social Work Education*, Working Paper in Sociology No. 11 (Durham).

Kogan, M. and Terry, P. (1971) *The Organisation of a Social Services Department* (London: Bookstall Publications).

Labour Party (1963) *Report on 1963 Labour Party Conference* (London: Transport House).

Leonard, P. (1979) 'Restructuring the Welfare State', *Marxism Today* (December 1979).

Longford Report (1964) *Crime: a Challenge to us All* (London: Labour Party Study Group).

Liverpool's Inner Area Study (1976) *Fourth Study Review* (Liverpool City Council).

Lyon, A. (1974) Quoted in Hansard, 29 July.

Mao Tse-tung (1973) *On Practice* (Peking: Foreign Language Press).

Parry, Noel, *et al.* (1979) *Social Work, Welfare and the State* (London: Arnold).

Poulantzas, N. (1978) *State, Power, Socialism* (London: New Left Books).

Pearson, Geoffrey (1975) *The Deviant Imagination* (London: Macmillan).

Robinson, G. (1978) 'How the Ruling Class Rules', *Marxism Today* (July 1978).

Shore, P. (1976) Quoted in Hansard, September.

Sinfield, A. (1969) *Which Way for Social Work?* (London: Fabian Society).

Social Workers Action Group (1979) *Social Services in Leeds* (Leeds Local Authority Branch, NALGO).

Specht, H. (1975) *Community Development in the UK* (London: Association of Community Workers).

Stein, M. (1979) 'Children of the State', *Social Work Today* (March).

Urban Deprivation Unit (1975), Note, 4 July.